D0831681

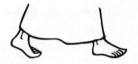

WAYS OF PRAYER SERIES

Basil Pennington, OCSO

Consulting Editor

Volume 6

The Holy Mountain

Approaches to the Mystery of Prayer

by

Noel Dermot O'Donoghue, O.D.C.

261
O'D

Michael Glazier, Inc.
Wilmington, Delaware

ABOUT THE AUTHOR

Noel Dermot O'Donoghue, O.D.C., is a teaching member of the Faculty of Divinity of the University of Edinburg, being the first Catholic to obtain a full teaching post in a Scottish Faculty of Theology since the Reformation. He has a doctorate in philosophy from the University of Louvain. He has published about a hundred articles in various scholarly, pastoral and spiritual journals, and a collection of these articles in a book entitled *Heaven in Ordinarie.*

Published in 1983 by: MICHAEL GLAZIER, INC. 1723 Delaware Avenue, Wilmington, Delaware 19806 and Dominican Publications, St. Saviour's, Dublin, Ireland.

Library of Congress Catalog Card Number: 82-84411
International Standard Book Number:
  Ways of Prayer series: 0-89453-282-0
  THE HOLY MOUNTAIN:
    0-89453-300-2 (Michael Glazier, Inc.)

Cover design by Lillian Brulc
Typography by Peg McCormick
Printed in the United States of America

CONTENTS

1. The Vision of the Mountain 7

2. Christ in the Contemplative Tradition 18

3. Space and the Spirit: A Mediation on Prayer in the
   Acts of the Apostles 33

4. Prayer and the Priesthood 44

5. Prayer and the Future 58

6. Community of Forgiveness 70

7. The Fourth Liberation: Self-Relinquishment in the
   Cloud of Unknowing and the *Epistle of the Privy
   Counsel* 92

8. The Sword of Peace: Some Reflections on
   Christian Pacifism 121

9. The Place of the Angels 126

10. Sister Death 142

11. Something Understood: Reflections on the Future
    of Academic Theology 174

ACKNOWLEDGEMENTS

Chapter 2 (Christ in the Contemplative Tradition) appeared in *The Furrow* (Maynooth) as part of a series of articles on Contemplative Prayer. Chapter 3 (Space and the Spirit) is the text of a talk given in May 1982 to the Iona Prayer Group in Stirling. Chapter 4 (Prayer and the Priesthood) is the text of a talk given to the Maynooth Union Summer School, June 1981. Chapter 5 (Prayer and the Future) is the text of a talk given to the past pupils of the Catechetical Institute of Mount Oliver Dundalk, Ireland; it has already appeared in *The Church in 2001* (Ed. Brady, Dominican Publications, Dublin, 1982). Chapter 6 (Community of Forgiveness) was given as a symposium talk at Spode House, May 1979, and appeared in the Supplement to *Doctrine and Life*, December 1979. Chapter 7 (The Fourth Liberation) appeared in the *Journal of Studies in Mysticism* (Autumn, 1979) under the title: "This Noble Noughting and this High Alling". Chapter 8 (The Sword of Peace) was presented as part of a "Peace Day" conference in the 1981/82 Session of the Faculty of Divinity of the University of Edinburgh in March, 1982. Chapter 9 (The Place of the Angels) was part of a conference on "The Spirit-World" which took place at the Salisbury Centre, Edinburgh, in 1980. Chapter 10 (Sister Death) appeared in *The Furrow*, June 1979, as part of a series by various authors. Chapter 11 (Something Understood) is the text of the opening lecture of the 1981/82 Session of the Faculty of Divinity of the University of Edinburgh.

Acknowledgement is made to the following for use of copyright material: Hamish Hamilton for quotations from *The Lost Country* by Kathleen Raine. Burns and Oates for quotations from *The World of Persons* by C. Winckelmans de Cléty and for the use of the McCann edition of *The Cloud of Unknowing*. Anthony Fleming for use of the Reynolds translation of Canto 33 of Dante's *Il Paradiso*. (C/o Penguin Books Ltd., Harmondsworth, Middlesex, England.) Faber and Faber for the quotation from T. S. Eliot's *Four Quartets*. Rosemary Haughton for the quotation from "Discovering Community". (Unpublished). The Delegates of the Oxford U.P. and the Syndics of the Cambridge U.P. for quotations from The New English Bible. *The Scotsman* (Edinburgh) for the report quoted from the issue of June 9th, 1980. The Estate of Alexander Carmichael for the Gaelic version of "Michael, the Victorious".

1

The Vision of the Mountain

In both the Old and the New Testaments the mountain is a place of prayer, the place of the encounter of man with God. It was on Mount Horeb that Moses met the angel in the burning bush and heard the voice of God and the name of God as "I am" or "I am He who Is". (*Exodus* 3). It was on Mount Carmel that Elias challenged and defeated the prophets of Baal, and established again the cult of the God of Abraham and Moses (I *Kings* 18). These two mountain experiences are united in the story of the transfiguration, when Jesus goes with three of his disciples into "a high mountain where they were alone" (*Matt.* 17, 1) and is shown in his transfigured brightness speaking with Moses and Elias. Luke, who shows Jesus at prayer in all the great "passages" of his life, begins his account of the Transfiguration by saying that Jesus "went into the hills to pray", and goes on to say that the "change" took place "while he was at prayer" (*Luke* 9, 28).

The mountain is at once the desert and the altar, the *altare*, the elevation where man encounters the divine mystery. In the valleys and the plains are the dwellings of man with all the turmoil and destruction, the mistakes and ambiguities, the cruelties and hypocrisies, of the human story. There also men and women cry out for deliverance; there the captives wait in bondage; there the poor are exploited and dehumanised by the wealthy; there the dark powers have their empire. To go to the mountain is to leave this world behind and to open to the countenance of God, to the face of the Father, the Source of all Truth, Life, and Beauty.

The mountain is also the place of silence, indeed the place of many silences, as those who have lived among the mountains well know. The silence of noon among the mountains is one thing, and the silence of midnight another; so too there is the silence of dawn which sometimes touches Shakespeare's troubled heroes and gives them peace, and the silence of sunset so beloved of Virgil as he speaks of "the long shadows falling across the high hills". There is the silence of high summer and of brooding winter, of awakening spring and autumn passing gently into that sleep of nature in which, nevertheless, the spirit of the earth seems most alive and awake. Within each of these silences the creative word is spoken. "Jesus Christ, who is the Word of God, came forth out of silence", says Ignatius of Antioch.[1] In silence the word travelled across the holy hills of Palestine as Mary went to meet Elizabeth. In the Carmelite tradition Mary is closely connected with Carmel, the mountain of Elias. She is the woman of prayer, who ponders the

---

[1] Magnesians 8,2. Quoted by J. Jeremias in *The Central Message of the New Testament*, SCM Press, 1965, p. 88.

Christ-mystery in her heart (*Luke* 2, 19 and 51), and Carmel is the mountain of prayer where the Lord manifests his presence with elementary power: in fire, air, earth and water; in smoke and cloud; in the sacrificial flowing of blood. The altar of sacrifice, in the Old Covenant and the New, is but a symbol of the mountain, the place of prayer and of the divine encounter. What the human father is for the child who says "Abba, abba" as it comes out of the silence of birth, the mountain is for the man who looks up to the Lord and dares to speak with him in full familiarity. The life of Jesus is the story of the fullest and deepest expressions of the Abba-prayer. On the mount of Calvary, he could finally and fully commend his whole being to the Father. He himself had become the Holy Mountain, from which flow the streams of salvation.

All these symbols do but point to the hidden mysteries of prayer, and all that is set down in the following pages is an exploration, or series of explorations, of this mystery. Each chapter is a fresh expedition into the hills; each is an answer to the challenge of the inaccessible summit of the Holy Mountain; each attempts a kind of breakthrough, seeking insight, seeking understanding.

Each expedition seeks the Face of the Living God, either alone or in the company of the seekers of the past: prophets, evangelists, mystics, theologians, philosophers, poets. The company is a large one, and there is a sense in which no human witness can be excluded, for even those who *obviously* point in the wrong direction are witnesses to the right direction. Besides — and this is the important point — the way to the Face of God is by way of the Face of Man. It is by the exploration of human dimensions — an exploration already carried some distance in a previous book — that the divine dimensions are revealed.[2] The surest way to the diminishment of the divine is the diminishment of the human. A high theology which largely ignores the works of man (art, poetry, philosophy, history) ends up by destroying the works of God: the Totally Other becomes the Totally Absent, like the God of the priests of Baal on Mount Carmel.

If there is — as I am convinced there is — an Adversary who tries to possess man and man's world and bring it under his power, then this Adversary will work not only or primarily by oppressing God or man's faith in God *directly*, but by persuading man that the human as such is without value or dignity. One thinks immediately of the psychological reductionism of Freud and Skinner, but the main attack on man today comes from theology and philosophy. Most theologians nowadays claim to have left the world of Karl Barth behind them, yet it is being brought home to me constantly how much both Protestant *and* Catholic theology lives in the shadow of Barth's anti-humanism: one clear sign of this is the rejection of Natural Theology and of Ethics as moral *philosophy*. On the side of philosophy the prevailing "death of man" and "death of system" philosophies of Michel Foucault and Jacques Derrida seems to me far more destructive than the atheistic humanism of Sartre or Heidegger. In the English-speaking world Analytical Philosophy has been generally destructive of the human, not so much directly as by its atmosphere of grey neutrality, its reduction of all questions to a common level of triviality. But, of course, the great anti-human force, the great attack on the Heart of God by the destruction of the heart of man is that Totalitarianism in

[2]*Heaven in Ordinarie*, T. & T. Clark, Edinburgh, 1979; Templegate, Springfield, Ill. 1979.

which the individual person is dissolved in the collectivity. Here as elsewhere the Adversary takes the appearance of an angel of light, or more exactly wears the "angelic" masks of truth, justice, and peace. In our day this mask has begun to slip, and the Hungarian, Polish, and South American experiences have shown the naked face of the Adversary of man and God.

So it is that these explorations of the mystery of prayer are in various ways explorations of the riches and resources of the human. Even the "dark companions" of human life, companions such as pain and death, are seen as horizons of man's destiny and possibilities. One can accept that men and women are born under the shadow of what is called "original sin" without denying or questioning the goodness and greatness of the human in *all* its energies and dimensions. The heart of man is troubled and the mind of man confused, not because of what he lacks but because of what he has; it is the New Man within him seeking to be born that troubles him. Most Reform theologies and most contemporary Catholic theologies tend to see the New Man as discontinuous with natural, "fallen" man. Again I see this attitude as destructive of the human and ultimately of the divine: it leaves us with a fantasy God playing with a fantasy man. Like all fantasy figures these are supremely manageable, and the theologian lives a beautifully insulated existence as a theologian. He pitches his tent comfortably at the foot of the Mountain and regales the would-be climber with "tales of the unknown" as a substitute for the great adventure that calls him to the holy heights.

At the centre of the *humanum* (the human in all its dimensions) is the phenomenon of human love in its dual aspect of *eros* and *agape.* At the centre of the exploration that follows is the theme of the unity of these forces, but this unity is not seen as cheaply available. Rather is it a hard-won achievement, an achievement never beyond question. This achievement is in a sense the whole meaning of mystical prayer, and the humanism based on this achievement can only be a *mystical* humanism. This mystical humanism is one of the horizons of this study, a horizon constantly glimpsed but never fully explored. For this exploration needs a new language, and I am not sure if this language can be created or discovered in our generation. Certainly it can only be truly heard in the silence of the Holy Mountain.

Every pathway that truly leads into this Mountain is a way of liberation, social, political, above all personal. If I try to liberate others without first liberating myself, I will end by binding them into my own bondage. So it is that the theme of personal liberation surfaces again and again, and the theme of social and political liberation takes a lower place. This must not be taken to mean that the man who prays on the mountain is forgetful of social and political dimensions. Rather he is too acutely conscious of these dimensions to attach himself to superficial solutions and incomplete revolutions.

It is from the Holy Mountain that the true solution of man's problems and the complete over turning of oppression is preached. The Woman who carried the Word over the hills of Judea was full of thoughts of revolution, and she expresses these thoughts when she comes to the end of her journey: "He has cast down the mighty from their seats and has exalted the lowly" (*Luke* 1, 52). This is not the substitution of one set of top people for another, but rather the radical rejection of the very principle and criterion by which such valuations are made. When the Word of God is born and manifested to men

and women, it affirms this radical overturning, this "catastrophe" in what we know as the Sermon on the Mount. (*Matt.*
5 to 7). For anyone who takes it at all seriously, this Word on
the Mountain is full of hard sayings, sayings which can be
heard only in the silence of prayer and the prayer of silence.

Some of the chapters that follow are experiments in *listening*
to the Word on the Mountain, the Word of Peace that is the
Sword of Peace. They try to create a space in which radical
pacifism may begin to inhabit the earth. There is a close link
between this theme and the theme of the unity of *eros* and
agapé, for men and women have finally no space within
themselves in which the word of peace may be received and
may grow to maturity except that creative love which guards
all procreation, all sympathy and compassion, all true art and
philosophy. This is "the great mystery" of which St. Paul
speaks (*Eph.* 5, 32) in which the heart of woman and the heart
of man are one, the mystery of the Woman clothed with the
Sun (*Apoc.* 12).

It is well to distinguish between the theologically important
question of *discernment* and the philosophically important
question of *availability.* In the case of every visionary, whether
it be St. Paul, or St. Teresa, or Nostradamus, or the Rev. Sun
Myeung Moon, there is question of discerning the status and
value of the experience of the "seer": it may all come from
fantasy or subconscious pressures, or from some evil or
mischievous spirit. I have not been directly concerned with
questions of discernment when the visionary theme surfaces
in these explorations, though I have touched on some principles of caution when speaking of the phenomenon of the
"trapped light" in the chapter on "Prayer and the Future". On
the question of the availability of an inner world or worlds I

have, however, taken a strong line. By availability I mean simply that experiences of other regions of reality than the visible-physical may well be true, are not necessarily false. I mean that the door is not closed to experiences which are neither physical in the usual sense nor yet purely spiritual.

It was Descartes who divided the world firmly into two regions, thinking or "spirit" being and extended or "matter" being, and this division rules out other regions. Recently there has been much discussion on the place of imagination in theology, but those who take part in these explorations tend to avoid the question as to whether there is a kind of human imagination which *discovers* a region of reality that it neither matter nor spirit in the Cartesian sense. It seems to me that everybody before the time of Descartes assumed that there were such intermediary regions of being, regions inhabited by "angels" and "archetypes", and the barely discernible lineaments of the Kingdom of Heaven. I have explored this matter at various points in the pages that follow and I try to defend the availability of these regions and the reality of the beings that inhabit them. In all this I am, in Kathleen Raine's words "defending ancient springs", those visionary springs from which the writers of the Old and New Testaments have drawn abundantly.

According to this vision the archetype or prototype reveals itself behind the persons, objects, events, and locations of common day. So it is that Isaiah can speak of Calvary; so it is that the Virgin already brings forth the child of promise; so it is that the Paschal Lamb, the Lamb of God, and the Lamb that is adored in the Apocalypse, are one. It is only through the archetypal vision that the manifold of space and time can be understood, just as it is only the man who has grasped *the idea* of justice who can truly judge the justice of personal and political transactions. In our own day some imaginative writers have tried to recover the vision of the archetypes. James Joyce's two major works, *Ulysses* and *Finnegans Wake* are devoted to the exploration of the archetypal man; Charles Williams has ventured into the world of the animal archetypes, especially in *The Place of the Lion;* and C.S. Lewis and Tolkein are much more influenced by Williams' archetypal thinking than either is willing to admit.

Joyce works with many subordinate archetypes such as that of the River, which is not the Liffey but Anna Livia Plurabelle, all rivers and every river. This Archetype of the River goes back to Genesis and Homer and beyond. It is in this context and this tradition that one can speak of the Holy Mountain, at once all mountains and every mountain. This Mountain is the place of the offering up of prayer and sacrifice and the place of the coming down of the divine presence and wisdom. It is what Kathleen Raine calls "the mountain behind the mountain". It is the place of theophany, the place of advent and proclamation. "How beautiful on the mountains are the feet of one who brings good news, who heralds peace, brings happiness, proclaims salvation." (*Isaiah* 52, 7 J.B.) But the divine pierces man, breaks through his selfishness and possessiveness, breaks open his heart. It will destroy him unless he somehow presents himself, offers himself, opens some kind of holy space around himself. That is the meaning of sacrifice, which is bound up with the archetype of the Blood as the first outpouring of creative life. So it is right that the Lamb of God should be sacrificed on a mountain, on a high place by the city set on the Holy Mountain of Sion. One of the main themes of the present book is that the sacrificial act of

Calvary was and is an *act, an activity,* a prayer. Jesus prayed his death as he had prayed his life.

Through his encounter with the Living God on the Holy Mountain Moses received the clarity and strength to speak out against the injustices and hypocrisies of his time. So too Elias, the man "consumed with zeal for the Lord God of hosts", spoke out on Mount Carmel against the priests of Baal, who had taken over the whole land and polluted the springs of sacred ritual. The man who goes to meet the Living God on the Mountain is not afraid to speak the truth, not afraid to wield the Sword of Peace. If he is a Christian he has met the Christ of the Sermon on the Mount, and he knows that the words of non-violent "catastrophe" come from the heart of the Mountain. He is the knight-errant of this Christian catastrophe: the overturning of all the values of the world and its leaders. He comes not to bring peace but the sword.

This however is but the externalisation of something that has its true power in another region, that inner region where the real battle rages, where Michael and his angels fight against the Dragon and his angels. (*Revelation* 12, 7). Here in this ancient conflict we take our stand, having within us the "new life" which flows from Calvary. But we need to make this life more and more our own; we need to let our own life-blood flow out in renunciation and sacrifice in order that the Christ-life may find new channels. We need to assimilate the mystery into the depths of our earthly existence in order that this mystery should more and more widely and deeply transform the earth. This is the work the man and woman of prayer are called to do. This is the cosmic meaning of the Holy Mountain.

Finally, the Holy Mountain contains within its peaks and valleys places sacred to joy and laughter, and this has its echoes everywhere. A certain ponderous dullness and flatness of style is an infallible sign that a writer is not a true guide to the sacred places. There must be a life in the writing that tells of Inner Life. All that follows has brought continued joy in the writing, a joy never far from the springs of laughter. Even though the dark ikon of Christ crucified could have been put on the cover of this book, yet that ikon has another side, that of a child full of the joy of eternal innocence. And the lineaments of the one are always showing through the lineaments of the other. The Holy Mountain is always both Calvary and Thabor; it is also the place of the coming of the Lord and all that this means of breaking and remaking for man and woman. But the Lord comes also and ultimately in the joy and deliverance and the peace that is beyond all price and understanding.

2

Christ in the Contemplative Tradition

The Christian contemplative tradition begins in the New Testament, which is at its deepest level a series of meditations on the death-for-love and life-for-salvation of Jesus of Nazareth, the anointed Son of Man, who is recognized as Son of God. All Christian contemplation reaffirms, and tries to recapture, this original vision. There is, of course, development, variety, individual testimony, so that the total Christ will speak with a voice like the sound of many waters (Rev. 1:16). But the voice of the source speaks in all its derivations.

It is the one sound, the one voice, and in a sense, any New Testament text will do to express it. Yet here and there it issues forth with special clarity and I want to make this chapter a kind of listening to one such text, one which has haunted the consciousness of Christians like the snatch of a song heard in childhood.

The text is from St. Paul, from that strange passionate Letter to the Galatians where he is, as it were, fighting for his life as an Apostle, and not for *his* life alone, but for *the* life, the new life that he carries within him, and wants to share with the whole world. The text runs as follows:

> I have been crucified with Christ; the life I now live is not my life, but the life which Christ lives in me and my present bodily life is lived by faith in the Son of God, who loved me and sacrificed himself for me.[1]

Here already we have the three modes of Christ-presence in the contemplative life which the subsequent history of Christian spirituality was to differentiate, develop, and sometimes distort and destroy: identity, imitation, and espousal. The first is clearly stated in this text; the others are in the background but really present nevertheless. From the point of view of proximity the order would be: imitation, espousal, identity; and it is in this order I shall deal with them.

---

[1]Gal. 2:20-21. This is the NEB translation, which is sufficiently clear and close to the Greek for our purpose, though it will be necessary to try to weigh and sift the Greek original in places. One main theme, perhaps *the* main theme, of Galatians is the contrast between the Way of the Law and the Way of the Cross: the Law was a kind of temporary tent in enemy country, the Cross was the total defeat of the enemy in Christ. The task of the Christian is to appropriate this victory by embracing the Cross of Christ; the "senseless" Galatians had gone back to the "safety" of the Law, and so were turning away from the life and freedom of Christ. They must open their eyes, regain their vision, enter into the contemplation of Christ crucified, and so walk in freedom.

The Imitation of Christ

Some years ago the Existentialist philosophers were saying that man is freedom; today the Structuralist or "death of man" philosophers are saying that man dissolves under analysis into the structures that shape him, or in other words, that man is a centre of imitation. Perhaps it may be possible to bring the two conceptions together by saying that man is at once freedom and imitation, that in every man these two dimensions somehow intersect. I am free to choose the models I will follow, the masters I will study, the voices I will heed, the way I will go. But I cannot escape all imitation, for even the words I use are signs and sounds which I imitate. I may, like Robert Frost, choose "the less travelled road", but some at least have travelled it before me. I may even choose to be a complete oddity, but even here I have my companions. I can choose what to imitate or whom to imitate; I cannot choose not to imitate.

Imitation and choice are in fact main themes in the Letter to the Galatians, and they appear clearly in the passage I have chosen. "I have been crucified with Christ", says Paul, meaning that this is the way he has chosen, that this is not the way his opponents have chosen, that this is the only way that leads to what he calls justification or righteousness (*dikaiosynē*). The shadow of the *stauros,* the Cross, lies over this text, as it lies across the whole of the New Testament. It is in the light of the *stauros* that a man is tested at the very centre of his freedom. What is tested, what is revealed is not whether a man accepts or rejects the *stauros* but whether he really accepts it for himself, as entering into his own personal life. Any doctrine of either faith or works that side-steps or obscures this issue is missing the point. The point is so sharp and pierces so deep that the history of Christianity is largely a history of more or less sophisticated efforts at avoiding it, or blunting it, or weakening its force or penetration. The Letter to the Galatians is simply an effort to meet one of the first of these evasions.

But what does it mean, this imitation of Christ crucified? Obviously it does not mean that Paul (or the true disciple) is literally crucified, or is even facing the decision to accept physical crucifixion. Neither does it mean that Paul is undergoing great physical sufferings or privations: there is no question of this kind of situation in the case of the Paul who writes this particular letter. What then is in question? There is question, as appears later, of the crucifixion of the lower nature, the *sarx*, "with its passions and desires" (5:24). There is question, more profoundly, of a certain attitude to the world, the *cosmos*; because he looks to the Cross Paul can say: "the world is crucified to me and I to the world" (6:14). The Cross confronts the *cosmos*, and the *cosmos* confronts the Cross; a man is faced with the choice of going one way or the other. St. Ignatius of Loyola was to reaffirm the radical challenge of this choice in his meditation on the "two standards". So, in the same period and in the same place did St. John of the Cross. So in another century and another place did St. Francis of Assisi. So did St. Bernard; so did St. Augustine. But, of course, this original call, this original clarifying challenge is echoed in every age, and in every place where the Gospel has been preached.

Because Paul (and the tradition that follows him) speaks of crucifying the lower nature, and of standing in opposition to the *cosmos*, it is easy to get the impression that the imitation of

Christ crucified is merely an ascetical journey. It is this of course; but it is much more, and it is in this much more that its essence lies. After all, one can imitate Moses, or Elias, or Socrates, in mastering the flesh and laying down one's life for truth and justice. The imitation of Christ belongs to another order. It is an opening, towards a new power, towards the substance of a new world, towards a new life. The *slauros* is seen as the sign of victory; on the Cross Christ had defeated the Lord of the *cosmos*. To look to the Cross is to open wide to this victory, to make it one's own. The work has been done; the victory has been gained. Luther saw clearly that all a man has to do is to establish living contact with this victory by way of faith. By looking to the Cross Luther corrected "the theology of glory" which would build an earthly kingdom of prelates and political power. He saw clearly the source of all grace. Where he made his tragic mistake was in seeing the role of the disciple as that of acceptance apart from imitation. Yet what Paul is saying here and elsewhere is that faith issues in imitation, in being crucified with Christ. The new life into which the disciple is called is not given in the mode of a gift in the hand, but in the mode of a sword that pierces the heart. This sword carries the charge of the new life; through it the Holy Spirit takes over and brings with it "the harvest of the Spirit" which is "love, joy, peace, patience, kindness, good-ness, fidelity, gentleness, self-control" (5:22). This is indeed a joyful harvest; and it gives the lie to those who see the way of the Cross as a way of doom and desolation.

The theme of the imitation of Christ is one of the constants of Christian spirituality East and West: the continuing popu-larity of books such as *The Imitation of Christ* is an indication of this; the article on the Subject in the *Dictionnaire de Spiritualité,* is a proof and illustration of it; the widespread interest in Charles de Foucauld (1858-1916), who made it the centre of his spirituality shows the continuing strength of its appeal to Christian consciousness. Strangely, both systematic and moral theologians tend to overlook it, and commentators on the New Testament rarely focus on it. Yet, in a real sense, it is neither more nor less than the theme of full discipleship, of the full following of Christ.

Christ the Bridegroom

In the source text already cited (Gal. 2:20, 21) — which is only one among many that could have been chosen to identify our theme at the source — we find the words: "my present bodily life is lived by faith in the Son of God, who loved me and sacrificed himself for me".The more one listens to this text and really hears it, the more clearly sounds the personal note. Christ loved me and gave himself up (*paradontos heauton*) for me. The title accorded to Christ, his highest title, Son of God, accentuates rather than diminishes the intimacy of this state-ment, while it reminds us also of the recurring theme of the glorification of man in Christ, the "hope of glory" (Col. 1:27). There is something here which is the hallmark of Christian spirituality, "the Emmanuel theme" it might be called: God comes down to where man is; God is with us, individually with me; "he that is mighty has done great things for me and holy is his name" (Luke 1:49). Christian prayer, Christian aspiration does not simply ascend, does not pierce the heavens to disappear into Nirvana; rather does it open to a descending heaven, a deity that pierces the earth and remains within it. This deity is indeed "a consuming fire" yet at the same time it is a deity with a human face, a human heart, human hands and feet pierced and flowing: the fire becomes the flowing of blood from a human heart.

So it is that one cannot listen for long to the resonances of this text without hearing the language of espousal and marriage, without realising that the great stream of bridal mysticism that marks the growth; the exuberances, exaggerations, pathology; the fervour and flowing heroism; the vicissitudes; the continuing presence of the Christian-feminine does indeed have its source in the source itself, in the New Testament. Again and again practical and prudent men have cleared it away in the name of building the earth or providing "sane and solid" doctrine for respectable folk and their children. But of course it always comes back. Christ refuses to be, primarily and for long, either Christus Rex or Christus Victor or any Christus-at-a-safe-distance. He is, first and last, Christ the Lover, the Bridegroom, the Spouse of the Soul.[2]

We are here in the inner sanctuary of Christianity, that Christianity of the heart which is, for a certain tradition, the heart of Christianity. It is a place of tenderness, a place of tears, the place of the Beloved Disciple, of Magdalen. A hymn such as *Jesu dulcis memoria*, with its haunting words and plangent melody, expresses best of all its poignancy and power. Yet this hymn of Jesus-Lord cannot be translated into modern English

---

[2]See the article entitled "The Spouse of the Soul" by Sacerdos, *The Furrow*, December 1961, especially the section on "The Song of St. Ita". It is worth noting that the word "soul" in the Christian mystical tradition is not really a dualistic concept but rather denominates the whole person as open to "the transforming union" with God.

without becoming curds and whey in the process. Neither is it possible to translate the sermons of St. Bernard, nor any of the medieval commentaries on the Song of Songs into present-day English. I do not know how such literature would fare or has fared in other twentieth-century vernaculars. Gaelic, insofar as it lives on, is still available as a voice for bridal piety; perhaps this is because Gaelic has not, as yet, lost its innocence.[3]

Because the language in which I write has lost its innocence it is extremely difficult to speak of the heart of Christ as the heart of Christianity. One has only to listen to any of the hymns or litanies of the Heart of Jesus — the Sacred Heart, to use the common term of Catholic devotion — to feel outraged in one's sense of language, or reverence, or both. And of course the statues and pictures are even worse. Speak of this great central devotion to any Protestant and he will say (or think), "Oh dear, you don't mean all those bleeding hearts". Yet it is my experience that there is no element in Christian devotional tradition for which young people today, Catholic or Protestant, are more eagerly seeking than that which centres on the Sacred Heart of Jesus and the Immaculate Heart of Mary. I am also convinced that this great world of divine life, this marvellous harmony of masculine and feminine is closed off from many pious Catholics by the very language and iconography that seek to express it.

I do not wish to exaggerate the difficulty. Christ, the Bridegroom radiates, however brokenly, through the interstices of congealed cliches, and dwells in the shadowed spaces of

---

[3]It is perhaps significant that Padraig Pearse's expressions of a quite innocent "socratic" affection for boys and appreciation of the physical beauty of boyhood, become in English translation pederastic. See A.D. Edwards, *Patrick Pearse*, Faber 1977, p. 127.

the oleographs. Yet there is a question of language, and the need "to purify the dialect of the tribe"; above all there is a need to recover the penumbra of the word, the *Logos* that shines through every *logos*, the dimensions hidden behind physical dimensions. The heart we name in the word "heart" is not simply the physical heart of anatomy and medicine, but rather the life heart and the feeling heart, and beyond all these the *self* heart that is the ultimate mystery of eternal spirit in temporal matter. So, too, blood, hand, head, the four elements: there is everywhere the archetypal, the penumbra that reveals the greatness of man, the vastness of the universe he inhabits, not just the physical world ruled by decay and death, but the other regions, the life-world, invisible *and yet not pure spirit,* the world of the Resurrection in which dwells not simply the Spirit of Jesus but his body. In a culture which accepts transcendence, which breathes the spirit-atmosphere, words open up towards these inner regions. "Did we not feel our hearts on fire as he talked with us?" said the disciples at Emmaus. What heart is this? What fire is this? Can we still speak in this way? Can we talk of the tender love of the Bride for the Bridegroom without either despiritualising our words or dematerialising them? Can we find again those lost human dimensions of spirit in matter?

If we do, *as* we do, we shall begin to discover the contemplative of the divine-human espousals. We shall have some oil in our lamps when the Bridegroom comes!

Christianus Alter Christus

"The Christian is another Christ". This ancient phrase may be understood in a wide variety of senses. It may mean simply discipleship, "the following of Christ", a walking of the path the Master walked. It may mean imitation, the "putting on" of Christ, the acceptance of the *stauros* into one's deepest being in the way explained above — indeed the author of the article in the *Dictionnaire de Spiritualité* already cited, "L'Imitation du Christ", uses the phrase in its imitational sense. The phrase may be weakened in the direction of metaphor (as for Shylock, in Shakespeare's *Merchant of Venice*, Portia is another Daniel). Or it may be strengthened in the direction of identity, so that the primary emphasis is not on the otherness (*alter*) but on the Christ-presence in the Christian. The Christian as such, as fully Christian, is Christ-possessed: Christ dwells in him, inhabits him.

It is in this strong sense that Paul sees himself as another Christ in our source text: "I live now not I but Christ lives in me" — *zō de ouketi egō, zē en emoi Christos.* We are in the region of life, of Zōē, a world that has within it two distinct but interpenetrating regions, the regions of life in the flesh (*en sarki*) and life in Christ. This latter is the region of "aeonic" life, the *Zōē aeonios* that is always near to mind in Paul and in John. A life lived in this region, a life whose centre of energy and force is in this region, is of a different substance from that of the corruptible stuff of "the world of this death". It belongs not to the side of *cosmos* (where an evil aeonic spirit reigns: 1:4) but to the side of heaven (*ouranos*).

The Christian has to dwell in the *cosmos* as Jesus Christ came to dwell in the *cosmos*, and it is true that the evil power, the *poneros* (1:4) has, as it were, wrested the cosmos from its proper alignment, and has established its special stronghold in man's flesh, in the region of fleshly appetites. But Paul does not say that this region is of itself evil; rather is it part of an occupied territory that waits for liberation (Romans 8:22). Those commentators who would make "the flesh" (*sarx*) stand for man-as-tending-towards-evil miss the whole point: the flesh (with its setting in nature) is not an evil place in man but a good place in man where the evil power has, so to speak, pitched its tent. So it is there, in that place, in the flesh, that the evil power had to be challenged and defeated. Christ, the Word made flesh (in the new immaculate conception of the flesh) moves in to the stronghold of the Prince of this World (John 14:31) asking men to allow him to come in, and warning them solemnly that only by receiving him in the flesh can they have life (John, 6). The cross, the *stauros*, is the centre of the enemy's stronghold, the heart of darkness, or rather the weapon by which the enemy would destroy this intolerable purity ("in me he has not anything", he whose whole power consists in *having*). This weapon, the Sword of Darkness and Destruction, the instrument of death, becomes transformed by the blood which it sheds into a Sword of Light and the Source of Spirit and Life (3:13; 5:25).

This is the life by which Paul lives. It is real; it is not a metaphor. It is "spiritual" life in the sense that it opens up to the world of spirit, and in the sense that it flows from the Holy Spirit; but in itself, essentially, it is physical life: it is "that which I now live in the flesh" (2:20). It is a real power of operation, the energy (*energeia*) by which Paul labours (Col.

1:29). It flows from the Cross, abundantly, yet is intimately wedded to the pain and affliction of the Cross, so that the disciple enters into the very activity of salvation, becomes himself a source of this life (Col. 1:24). There is no question of a facile drawing *from* the source; rather does the disciple find himself drawn *into* the source and sharing in the very "woundedness" of Christ (6:20). The death of Christ and all it entails is as much present in the disciple as the life of Christ and all it gives (2 Cor. 4:10).

We are here at the heart of the Christian spiritual tradition. Martyr, monk, minister, missionary: all draw from "the fountains of the Saviour", but all in the depth of their calling are drawn into the very source of these fountains: all are "other Christs". Grace, the gift of God, the indwelling of the Trinity, the "anointing" of the Holy Spirit, is not something merely given and thankfully received. It is this, but it is much more. It is a giving of the giving, a sharing of the sharing. It is not only "Jesus saves" or, "Jesus is my personal saviour". Rather is it, "I am Jesus saving", "Jesus saving saves in me". Herein is the call to martyrdom, to the total self-giving of celibacy or the total detachment from family ties. In this way lies the desert, and the lonely mountain places; along this road lies Thabor, and Gethsemane. Not only faith, not merely imitation at some distance, not alone espousal and companionship, but through all this, a reaching beyond it, for man and woman, the identity with Jesus-Saviour, the initiation into Christ-anointing. It is this challenge and stretch towards the fullness of Christ that gives tension and vitality to the writings of the great witnesses to Christ: to St. Augustine, St. Bernard, St. Catherine, St. Teresa; to Abbot Marmion and St. Thérèse of Lisieux in modern times. It is this same challenge and stretch that distinguishes true Christ-identity from the way of the false Messiah and the neurotic. The latter pull the Christ-being into the narrow limits of their own ego; true Christ-identity calls the self beyond the self, always further and further into the Christ-infinity. There is no "perfection" here, no claim to "have arrived", but rather a journey into ever greater self-emptying as the "new life" establishes itself more and more completely. More compassion too, and more concern; for the Christed man or woman is ever more and more completely the one who belongs to others at all levels, personal, social, political, cosmic.

The Contemplative Church

So far I have been concerned mainly, though by no means exclusively, with the contemplative response of the individual Christian to Christ. The theme of "Christ in the Contemplative Tradition" can also be seen from an ecclesial or community standpoint. The pilgrim Church follows Christ along the path of the Passion and Death, the Resurrection and the Ascension, the final and total glory; already Paul spoke in so many words of the Christian community as the Bride of Christ, and this same theme is central to the Revelation of John; as for identity there is the mysterious and challenging figure of the Church as the Body of which Christ is the Head, and the hints of a "filling up" that has to be accomplished, a completion of the number (the "elect", or "predestined" number), not of those saved by Christ (for this is as wide as creation in the Divine plan as clearly stated in 1 Timothy 2:4), but of those brought into the saving work of Christ, the community of "other Christs" of "Christ-saviours". Thus we have at the community level as at that of the individual Christian the three-fold movement of imitation, espousal and identity. In the one eternal harmony each individual note mirrors the whole and enriches it. The expression of this harmony in the conditions of space and time, in the stress and strain of pilgrimage, in the varieties, vicissitudes, and ambiguities, of history is the liturgy of the Christian Church. Or to put it in another way, the Christian liturgy is related to Christian contemplation as the body is to the soul. What expresses itself in sacrament and sacrifice, in the public ministry of the word, in common prayer, is the community of loving, living contemplation of Christ, a community that culminates in Eucharistic Communion. Here, too, the Cross is at the centre, and the re-enactment of the self-giving of Christ on Calvary is for many Christian traditions the heart of the liturgy. In other traditions the altar becomes the table of communion and *agape*, in still others (in the case of the Quakers, for example) there is neither altar nor table, and shared space and silence embody the common contemplation of Christ. In all cases there is a shared contemplation of Christ as present in the community. In all cases Christ is not only or even primarily the object of contemplation; rather is he the *locus*, the presence within which the Divinity is encountered, the point of contact with the Mystery of God: Father, Son and Holy Spirit.

In our day the Christian liturgy has to contend with that "materialisation" of language of which I have already spoken. We hide our extreme poverty in this respect by constant recourse to Scripture, though much of our contemporary

understanding of Scripture (sometimes enshrined in translation) despiritualizes it. As miracles have been pushed aside, as
angels have disappeared, as the inner reality of water, fire,
blood, wine, bread and the rest have been reduced to metaphor, so gradually a certain spiritual atmosphere has been lost.
We need quite desperately a dematerialisation of language, a
return to innocence, the recovery of that penumbra by which
words are open to the sacred and mysterious.

But, of course, for the contemplative there is always silence,
that fulness of meaning beyond all words in which the spirit
listens with the inner ear and sees with the inner eye. All
liturgical prayer reaches up to this silence; all the words men
use to speak to Christ, or about him, or with him, open to that
infinite space in which the Word is always *with* God.

3

Space and the Spirit
A Meditation on Prayer in the
Acts of the Apostles

A Creative Explosion

In the *Acts of the Apostles* we see the Christ-power exploding into history. In the Gospels we witness the descent of this power into the very depths of this world and the kingdom of this darkness, and its mighty victory over that same darkness. According to an ancient and continuous tradition, the descent into the kingdom of darkness went down to the very depths of hell, to where immortal spirits were eternally bound by immortal hate. As below, so above: he who descended to the depths ascended to the heights "taking captivity captive". All this is accomplished through the power of the Spirit in the unity of the Father, Son, and Spirit.

The *Acts* opens with the dramatic account of the Ascension of Jesus (1:6 to 11). I see this as at once a historical event continuous with our every day experience and a prayer-event of the same quality as, or at least a similar quality to, the

Transfiguration. It is as if the disciples were taken some distance into the event itself, an event in which the everyday world opened out to an inner world or worlds, a world normally invisible but available to heightened awareness and extended perception. To this inner world belong the two men in white whom the disciples find standing beside them as the Risen Jesus disappears into a cloud, the cloud which serves normally as a bridge between the visible and the (normally) invisible world. These beings are clearly messengers or angels, and they or their fellow messengers will have a large part in subsequent events, releasing Peter from prison, bringing Philip to meet the Ethiopian and taking him away again, reassuring Paul in the midst of shipwreck (27:23). Unless we begin by allowing for the reality of this world of divine messengers and divine activity it is unlikely that we shall understand what is really happening in the *Acts*.

Let me return, however, to my first remark, that the *Acts* is an account of the explosion of the Christ-event into history. I mean, of course, a creative explosion, an explosion of new energy, new life, new relationships. The new energy is at once inapprehensible and palpable, universal and localised, always expected and always unexpected, fragrant as a rose-garden in bloom, yet keen and wild as the wind on the hills. It is nameless, yet it has a name, a very ancient name. It is the Breath of God, the *ruach*, the Holy Spirit.

Now the going of Jesus is closely connected with the coming of the Spirit. "If I do not go, the Paraclete will not come, whereas if I go I will send Him to you." (*John* 16:8). Yet as long as Jesus was with them the Spirit was with them: indeed it was through the Holy Spirit, says the author of *Acts*, that Jesus instructed them during the time between his Resurrection and Ascension (1:2). While he was with them he was the locus of the Spirit; when he left them and entered into the glory of the Father they became themselves the locus of the Spirit, and so, as time went on, conformed to his image. All those who came to them, who made real contact with them became part of the locus, that new temple, that new body in which the Spirit came to dwell. By baptism they were cleansed and prepared, by the imposition of hands they were filled: the *form* of contact did not matter, what mattered was the contact. There is a sense in which, then as now, the Spirit moves along the articulations of ritual initiation, and a sense in which the Spirit "blows where it wills", and meets every human spirit directly and uniquely.

One way or another the Spirit moves into a space which is ready to be filled. For all its fiery strength and creative power it cannot force its way in, cannot take over the heart that repels it, cannot share its dwelling with those dark cosmic forces which have found a place in men's hearts. It can indeed put those evil powers to flight, but only if the human heart welcomes it, and exposes itself to its radiance.

If we look carefully at the narrative of the *Acts* we shall see how the first Christian men and women provided the space for the Spirit, cooperated with that creative explosion whose background is the four Gospels, whose reverberations are the Letters of St. Paul and the other Apostles, whose culmination is the *Revelation* of John. *The Acts of the Apostles* is at once the story of this explosion, and the description of this space as it opened out by way of the mystery of personal and community prayer.

Inner and Outer Space

After the Ascension experience the disciples of Jesus returned to Jerusalem to wait for the coming of the Spirit according to the final instruction of Jesus as recorded by St. Luke. (*Luke* 24:49, *Acts* 1:4). It might seem at first sight that this time of waiting was a passive and empty time, but the author of *Acts* is at pains to emphasise that it is a time of active and intense inner preparation. He carefully distinguished three main groups who awaited the coming of the Spirit: the Apostles named one by one yet grouped as four, two, two and three; the women, who presumably include, if they are not identified with, "the women who followed Jesus from Galilee" of Luke's Gospel; finally Mary the Mother of Jesus and his brothers. I am not concerned with all the fascinating questions that arise as regards these groups, especially the second and third, but merely with noting how a community is already clearly defined, a nucleus from which the wider communities would open out. What I want to note is that this community, this first cell of the Church as it waits for Pentecost, is already a community of prayer, already a living space of invocation. "All these were constantly at prayer together." (*Acts* 1:14 NEB) *proskarterountes homothumadon en tḗ proseuchḗ.* The two Greek words by which this original community prayer is described are very strong, very significant, giving the sense of unity of heart and earnest striving. It must be remembered that we do not have here the sorrowful and frightened group to which Jesus had first appeared after the Resurrection, but rather a group full of the joy and light of the Risen Christ, for whom the ancient Scriptures had been marvellously opened and fulfilled. Nevertheless they were waiting for "the power from above" (*Luke* 24:49), and they were preparing within themselves the place of his coming. It is significant that they felt they had at this point to fill the space left vacant by Judas, as if the human space into which the Spirit would come should have a certain amplitude and structure. It is significant too that the group should be made up of women as well as men, and that Mary, the woman in whom the mystery of salvation had its beginning, should be present. In the first chapters of his gospel Luke had made it abundantly clear that Mary had a deep and wide interior life: "Mary treasured all these things and pondered over them" (*Luke* 2:19 and 51). Altogether we have a wide and deep human receptacle for the Coming of the Spirit.

But the Coming of the Spirit does not mean the end of prayer. Quite the contrary. For the Spirit is in the first place a guest received into the heart. It is in the words of St. John of the Cross, "a living flame of love". It is not the end of prayer but rather the fulfilment, as marriage is, at least ideally, the fulfilment of love. So it is that when the Apostles appoint deacons to serve at table, their reason is that they are called to devote themselves to prayer and the ministry of the Word. (*Acts* 6:5). Prayer is not simply a useful instrument in their preaching, nor yet the recognition of the needs of the community and the world. No, it is the service of a great love that has taken over their whole being. So it is that we find Peter stealing away to pray in quiet places, remaining there so long that he finds that he has grown hungry (10:10). So it is that Paul and Silas pray and sing the praises of the Lord while they are in an inner dungeon with their feet in the stocks. (16:24).

This prayer in captivity indicates an extraordinary paradox that runs through the whole account of the infant Christian community described in *Acts*. It is the paradox of contraction and expansion, the law that the more the first Christians were bound and gagged, hunted and imprisoned, the more that inner spiritual space expanded, the more widely the horizons of invocation opened up. The two leaders of the church are especially subjected to restraint and constriction: Peter and Paul are, as it were, singled out for beatings and imprisonment. It is precisely as this physical contraction is imposed that spiritual expansion is achieved. It is as if inner space were able to take over as outer space was obliterated. It is as if the utter constriction of Gethsemane and Calvary were being in a measure experienced again in the growing Body of Christ.

This law of contraction-expansion must be understood sensitively if we are to relate it to other circumstances and periods. People's lives may be constricted and stifled in ways other than prison and persecution, for instance, a man or woman may be effectively imprisoned by illness, one's own or another's. Moreover, Christian invocation as we encounter it in *Acts* is always breaking down prison doors and healing diseases. It is as if that inner spiritual space, as it is won and filled, flows outwards powerfully and refreshingly into the world of physical space. There is here a sense of liberation at all levels which comes across very powerfully in a passage in which we can imaginatively join that first Christian community at prayer.

The Place of the Trinity

The passage reads as follows in the *New English Bible* (Acts 4:23 following):

> As soon as Peter and John were discharged they went back to their friends and told them everything that the Chief Priests and Elders had said. When they heard it they raised their voices as one man and called upon God.
>
> Sovereign Lord, Maker of heaven and earth and sea and of everything in them, who by the Holy Spirit through the mouth of David thy servant, didst say, *Why did the Gentiles rage and the people lay their plots in vain? The kings of the earth took their stand and the rulers made common cause against the Lord and against his Messiah.* They did indeed make common cause in this very city against thy Holy Servant Jesus whom thou didst anoint as Messiah. Herod and Pontius Pilate conspired with the Gentiles and peoples of Israel to do all the things which, under thy hand and by thy decree were foreordained. And now, O Lord, mark their threats, and enable thy servants to speak thy word with all boldness. Stretch out thy hand to heal and cause signs and wonders to be done through the name of thy Holy Saviour Jesus.
>
> When they had ended their prayer, the building where they were assembled rocked, and all were filled with the Holy Spirit and spoke the Word of God with boldness.

This exultant prayer follows the astounding miracle of the healing of the crippled beggar at the temple gate. Peter and John were apprehended and brought before Annas and Caiaphas, where they spoke out boldly and had to be released because no charge could be found against them. So we have here a prayer of liberation: the cripple has been liberated, Peter and John have been liberated, above all the name of Jesus has been liberated. Yet for all that one realises, as they too must have realised, that the powers of darkness are still abroad, still powerful, still menacing, always waiting. It is no wonder that the thrust and power of that first prayer-consciousness affirmed the parousia of the Lord as a full and final liberation. Of course they did not fully realise that the space into which the returning Christ would come had to be won from the world of darkness slowly and painfully.

They are not without divine help in this task. Indeed this whole prayer is a recognition of the fact that, as the Gaelic proverb has it, the help of God is nearer than the door. For the space that is opened up is being constantly filled with the Spirit, and not only with the Spirit but with the Father as well and with his Son Jesus, risen and ascended. Indeed this prayer is fully Trinitarian, shows us the great central Christian doctrine where it most deeply belongs, in the clearing of Christian invocation, as experienced existentially and non-thematically. An existential experience is an experience as seen not in the phenomena that express it but in its source in the conscious subject. In our text the praying community is not making any thematic or dogmatic assertion about the Trinity; it is in a sense entirely pre-Trinitarian in its affirmations. Yet there is a triunity and threefoldness at the very source of this prayer of liberation expressed with such intensity by the little group of our forefathers in the faith. As we listen to the internal echoes and correspondences of this prayer we catch some of the power and poetry of this existential experience of the Father of earth and sea, the Son of man who was slain by man and rose again, and the ever-present, ever-mysterious Spirit who fills the human spirit and also fills the dwelling in which the spirit lives, not only the body of flesh and blood but the house of stones and wood and mortar.

Again it is prayer, this "togethering" prayer with its ancient formulae and its present concern, that opens up that space in the hearts of the disciples in which the Trinity or Triunity comes to dwell. Belief in the Trinity is not a doctrinal formula, necessary as this may be in certain contexts, but rather an opening of the human spirit to the Holy Spirit of truth and consolation. It is through the Spirit that the believer cries "Abba, Father" and affirms the name of Jesus, Saviour.[1]

Darkness and Light

In the fifth chapter of *Acts* the shadow of Satan falls across the page. We are told of a man who allowed Satan to possess his mind. Such is the contagion of evil that the man's wife is likewise persuaded by the dark power of greed and duplicity. And so we have the dramatic and chilling story of Ananias and Sapphira: man and wife are slain pitilessly and self-righteously by Peter, the same Peter who was rebuked by Jesus for wishing to call down fire from heaven on those who rejected the good news (*Matt.* 16:23). So, also, a little later, we find Paul striking a man blind who had opposed him: "mist and darkness came over him, and he groped for someone to take

[1]Using an ancient distinction we might say that these first Christians were believers in the Trinity not *in actu signato* (i.e. as a formulated position) but *in actu exercito* (as a lived experience).

him by the hand." (13:11). This is but a temporary punishment, whereas Ananias and Sapphira are given no real chance
of recovery or repentance.

It would seem that the Church lost its innocence at this
point, and has still to recover that innocence. Satan entered
the mind of Ananias in order to enter the mind of Peter. (Or if
you want to say that Luke made up the story as a cautionary
tale, then it is no less true that the mind of Luke has been
contaminated.) Peter had been given power to heal and
enlighten, not to punish and destroy. Jesus himself had the
power to punish and destroy, and he was tempted to use it
when Peter had suggested it. But that was not the will of the
Father who alone is entirely good and therefore shines like the
sun with equal goodness on all. There is certainly a "day of
reckoning", but that is simply the revelation of *how it is* with
people. And only the immutable and inaccessible light of the
Father is pure enough to show forth this final and unalterable
judgment.

One can indeed see the death of Ananias and Sapphira as a
severe mercy leading somehow to a better mind as they pass
through the portals of death. But this kind of softening of the
incident hardly meets the scandal of the violence and inhu-
manity of the text, and the haunting suspicion that the
shadow of Satan lies over Peter as well as the wretched pair
that are punished. And this leads me to my final observation
on the presence of prayer in the *Acts,* the observation that the
first Christian community is not, as we tend to think, pure
and innocent, but rather struggling towards purity and innocence, struggling towards clearing a space for the spirit of love.
The reception of the Holy Spirit is not a once-and-for-all event
of sanctification, but rather the dramatic initiation of a sancti-

fying process that is still going on. The Church is still today an invocational Church whose self-affirmation is firmly in the vocative mood: *veni Sancte Spiritus.* The Spirit has come to us to the extent of our receptivity. We are indeed filled with the Spirit, but how much of the shadow remains in us to connive with the surrounding darkness! In medieval theology the seven gifts of the Holy Spirit were seen as receptivities, modes of asking and receiving. It is this that some charismatic people have to learn today, that the Spirit leads us on and on into a world of ever-*widening* horizons and ever-*deepening* dedication, witness, charity, and — dare I say it — enthusiasm.

4

Prayer and Priesthood

First Mass

Many summers ago I said my first Mass here in Maynooth in the rather lovely oratory of St. Mary behind the High Altar in the famous College Chapel. I might add that according to the official list I was due to say my Mass somewhere in the windy cloisters, but at the last moment the senior sacristan changed his own plans so the last became the first, and there I was with my little group of relatives, albed and chasubled in the midst of the silver stars and shimmering blues of the Lady Chapel, *sacerdos in aeternum* albeit not quite yet nor indeed ever *sacerdos magnus,* for Holy Church decided that enough was enough, and never offered me a bishopric, either suppressed or merely oppressed.

So what was it all about, that event, little or great according to perspective, in which a young man of twenty-five surrounded by his family, mostly elders and betters (as one of

them quite frankly pointed out to him), put on strange clothes
and said words in a dead language, and offered up bread and
wine which, somehow, became the living Christ, Jesus of
Nazareth, who spoke of himself as the living bread that came
down from heaven? Was it merely ceremony and symbol
pointing to a great mystery? Or was it something more,
something literally earth-shattering in that it brought into that
world of space and time, the Lady Chapel, a little before noon
on 24 June 1946, a reality of another order, of another
substance that took the place of the substance of the bread and
the wine? For the ordinary priest working in an ordinary
parish this kind of questioning scarcely arises. And if he is
questioned, and is the dogmatical type, he has the answer pat:
transubstantiation is a fact vouched for by the Church, a fact
which is also a mystery, and that's the end of it. The honest
inquirer is just as baffled by this line as by the fundamentalist
Muslim's even more unbreakable affirmation that there is one
God and Mohammed is his prophet, or by the bright-eyed
youngster who tells us that Christ spoke to Mr. Moon and told
him to unite all Christian people under the banner of Mr.
Moon himself. This is what I call stonewall theology, and
though Catholic Dogmatics is less prone to it than most, yet
there is too much of it as long as there is any of it. True or
liberating theology is not a wall against unbelief, but a lamp to
illuminate belief for believers and unbelievers. Yet one cannot
go very far into transubstantiation theology without finding
oneself up against some stonewall assertion.

There is something more. Our people are, I would claim,
less and less concerned about transubstantiation, either to
grasp it (as an assertion) or to defend it. I am talking of what
are called practising Catholics. I do not know if the matter has

been studied much in America, Ireland, or Britain, but there is a French survey which claims that two out of every three church-going Catholics do not believe in the traditional doctrine, and see the Eucharist as primarily Christians sharing in the love of Christ and all it gives and demands. This is the attitude at Taizé, near Cluny in France, where the youth of the world come and go and spend three hours each day in common prayer.

I am raising these questions not because I want to engage in contemporary controversies such as that of Eucharistic hospitality, or because I want to open a discussion on Eucharistic theology, but because I want to see the Mass or Eucharist as part of the prayer-world of the priest, or more exactly to see the priest and his priesthood in terms of prayer. I want to see that event of years ago in the Lady Chapel as a prayer event within the great universe of prayer events that is as wide as creation. Here, as elsewhere, I want to "crack the code" of traditional formulae and see the unbroken continuity of theology with life.

The Springs of Salvation

It is generally accepted among Christian theologians that Christ came to save mankind. But when we try to focus more sharply the nature of this salvation and the way of its achievement we find many theological paths stretching before us. Some would say that Jesus shows men how to live and how to die as children of the Father. Others speak of justice and satisfaction: by his sacrificial life and death Jesus somehow paid the price of man's sin, restored the balance of justice. Some would see this debt as somehow owed to Satan, into whose power man had given himself by the sin of Adam. Original sin, however explained or left unexplained, has a large share in many theories of salvation: for some extreme Protestant thinkers man is in a state of total depravity until he is released and transformed by the grace of Christ. The concept of grace, which has a large place in St. Paul's thinking, is a fairly constant ingredient in both Catholic and Protestant theologies, and this mysterious entity is seen as something far above all human goodness and righteousness. Then there is the *Christus Victor* approach attributed to Luther by Gustav Aulén: Christ is the great hero who has broken the power of Satan and released man from this power.

One could add to this list according as one reads more books ancient and modern, and most of us will feel that for the most part what is being shown is a variety of sides of the same great building, or vistas of the same landscape. But there is one approach to the work of redemption that is not given a central place in any of the books and yet obviously deserves a central place: I mean the approach by way of the prayer of Christ. I would want to argue that Christ came to pray and to show us how to pray, and that it was by prayer that he saved mankind, and still saves mankind. Moreover I would want to argue not only that the priest is a man of prayer, but that prayer and priesthood are the one thing, that the priest is not only a man of prayer but the very presence of prayer among men. And I want to say that everything that occurred in the Lady Chapel on 24 June 1946 was prayer and nothing else.

The Prayer of Christ

How is one to express in a few words the height and depth of the dimension of the prayer of Christ? How can one show that Jesus of Nazareth was not a man who preached and worked miracles and died for man's salvation and who *also* prayed, but rather a man who prayed his life and prayed his death? How can one dare to challenge the order of priority of all Christian theology today and say to Barth and his followers, to Rahner, Küng, Schillebeeckx and the rest: your theology is lacking almost totally in that very colour which highlights the picture, you have failed to hear the keynote of that symphony which the Holy Spirit directs in the New Testament? All one can do is challenge one's hearers to read through the New Testament while opening the eyes and ears to this highlight and to this keynote. Or one can ask oneself whether the death on Calvary was an *activity* of Christ or something merely done to him: the clear answer that comes from a careful reading of the Passion narratives is that Jesus prayed his death, so much so that his death can only be properly understood as the culmination of the one continuous activity of prayer. The Lord's Prayer as we call it is not simply the prayer given by Jesus the Lord to his disciples; it is a window opened into the heart of a man who went off again and again to lonely places to pray, a man who spent whole nights in prayer, a man who built his new world not on Peter in the last resort, but on the prayer by which he himself upheld Peter. Only thus could the new world survive the sifting of Satan, the Prince of this World.

Peter can indeed be taken as the type of the priest, the man called into the mystery of the prayer of Christ, the man who is asked to confirm his brethren, to feed the sheep and the lambs. There are of course levels, and if you like, a hierarchy of service, but in Peter we surely have the priesthood in its pure essence, so that what is true for him is true for each one of us in our own place in the Lord's vineyard.

The Prayer of Peter

Let us then consider Simon Peter's relationship with the prayer of Jesus Christ. We know that the choice of Peter and the other apostles came after a whole night of prayer on the part of Jesus, so we can say that Peter's priesthood was born of prayer. It seems that for the most part Jesus went off alone to pray in desert places, but there are some occasions when Peter is present, on the fringe of the prayer of Jesus. This was so in the event of the Transfiguration which occurred, St. Luke tells us, while Jesus was at prayer. There Peter is quite overwhelmed and can only touch the experience in a broken, babbling fashion. At the other pole of the prayer experience of Jesus, that is to say in Gethsemane, Peter is also present, again on the fringe of the experience. He is also present during the priestly prayer of St. John's Gospel, where again a window opens into the heart of Jesus at prayer. And of course he is present at Calvary, again very much on the fringe of the event. In the Acts he is presented quite clearly as a man of prayer, a man for whom prayer comes first in the exercise of his apostleship. Finally, he too is crucified at the end, and so finally enters into the fulness of the prayer of Jesus. He became the broken bread; he drank the cup.

The Prayer of the Priest

We must tread softly here, for we are at the threshold of the sanctuary, within the *temenos* of the mystery. Into this sanctuary the young priest walks to gather the whole mystery into the words and gestures of what we know as the Mass. So much is gathered into this simple ritual, so much is placed upon the altar, the whole of history *teste* David Jones in his *Anathemata*. But the centre of it, or rather the vital energy that fills the sanctuary, is the prayer of Christ and the presence of Christ in that prayer. This presence is as real, as substantial, as the prayer is real and substantial. The young priest has not as yet attained to the dimensions of this prayer and any more than Peter had on Thabor or in Gethsemane. But he has, however, tremblingly, even foolishly, responded to this call to pray with Christ, and here he is most fully involved in this prayer. He does not at all realise that he is as yet a babe in arms, that he is being carried by the prayer of Christ and the Church, perhaps by the prayer of some of those who are his flock. As time goes on he will learn all this, and will come to admire the courage of Peter even when he could but touch the fringes of the mystery. So his making is an unmaking, his knowing an unknowing, and his breaking of the bread more and more a breaking of himself, so that he too may follow his Master into the glory of the Resurrection. The mark or *signum*, the *character*, as it used to be called, of his priesthood is the sign of the Cross, the sign of the radiant Cross of the Resurrection.

The Eucharist As Prayer

What then does he accomplish when he takes the bread and wine and pronounces what are called the words of consecration? What did Peter accomplish when he re-enacted the Lord's Supper among the first disciples? We can answer this only if we can say what the prayer of Christ and prayer in and with Christ accomplishes. Only if prayer is real and inhabits a world of reality is the Eucharistic prayer real in its affirmation of the real presence of Christ in the bread and wine.

There is a sense in which the eucharistic prayer of Jesus at the Last Supper is the culmination of a long, deep, demanding, all-consuming diaiogue with the Father, all that went into and came forth from those nights of prayer in lonely places. By this prayer, in and through his prayer, Jesus was earthing the divine in the world, the human world of love and hate, of desire and fear, of food and drink. In his physical being Jesus had become totally absorbed into the stuff of heaven, of that *ouranos* where the Father dwells. This would have been a relatively easy process for Jesus as a great mystic: indeed it may well be that others have achieved it and still achieve it. It was not to such people that Jesus came, not to the just but to sinners, to those held captive by the physical, held in the power of the Prince of this World. So it was that he who ascended in prayer, and became perfectly absorbed into the heavenly substance, chose to come down like manna, to descend into the physical world which held fast-bound the great majority of men. Only by absorbing him could they have the *aeonic* life of *ouranos.* "Unless you eat the flesh of the Son of

Man you shall not have life in you. I am the bread of life" (Jn. 6:35 and 53). Thus Jesus totally absorbed in prayer becomes the new life for men. But this could not be unless Jesus immersed himself completely in the flesh, and in so doing came under the terrible power of Satan. This was the final baptism, baptism in the earth, far more terrible than baptism in water. So his prayer became agony; his blood flowed freely into the cosmos. So it was that he could take bread and say "*this is my body*"; so it was that he could take wine and say, "*this is my blood*" (Mk. 14:22). So it is that a man can do this in his name, and know that a mighty change has been named and reaffirmed. So it is that every eucharistic celebration continues the prayer of Christ as he enters into the cosmos of pain and disease and all the works of Satan. Each eucharistic celebration extends the radiance of the death-prayer of Christ until he comes in glory, to claim what is his and leave behind, with unimaginable sadness, what is not his, the spirits that have fallen down into the kingdom of Satan.[1]

The words of consecration are part of the prayer of Christ as he prays a new world into being, a new heaven and a new earth. They are not a magic formula achieving a magic change; rather do they express here and now that planetary transformation at an unseen but utterly real level which flowed immediately from the destruction of death by the prayer of Christ that survived death, that took death into itself. As physical phenomena the bread and wine do not change any more than the physical phenomena of the planet changed at the death of Christ. But the earth changed in its inner

[1] Unless we take into account what Julian of Norwich calls "The Great Deed," see O'Donaghue *Heaven In Ordinarie* (T. and T. Clark, Edinburgh; Templegate, Springfield, ILL. 1979) pp. 156, 157.

substance, so that all bread is Christ's body and all wine is his blood, bread and wine and all that sustains man and supports him. All is instinct with the power and presence of Christ. When the priest says *"this is my body"*, *"this is my blood"*, he touches that vibrant life that pulses through the earth so that it comes to the surface as the hidden existence of this bread and this wine. This we call transubstantiation, for the underlying reality or *substantia* is changed.[2] Some Christian liturgies see

[2]It will be seen that I am here affirming *transubstantiation* in the traditional Catholic sense. In a nominalistic or conceptualistic era, when concepts are seen as no more than the building-bricks of mental constructions, the concept of "substance" seems no more than a left-over from a defunct philosophy. For the medievals, however, as for the Greeks, "substance" like other metaphysical concepts, indeed like all concepts, were centres of illumination, points of light, luminosities. These thinkers stood in the radiance of the Transcendentals (being, unity, truth, goodness), ultimately of the *divine* radiance. This was not a theological presupposition but a profound metaphysical insight: it faded gradually with the emergence of scientific humanism in the sixteenth century. Descartes had to find the source of light within the thinking subject. From this development, necessary in its way, in the *earthing* of human consciousness, came Kantian Idealism and (later) the Phenomenology of Husserl and the Existentialists; another development of scientific humanism rejected Descartes' inner light of consciousness and simply reduced all thought to sense perception — this has generated various forms of empiricism, the latest being what is called Linguistic Analysis or, more simply, Analysis. (For a powerful critique of this development see *The Limits of Analysis* by Stanley Rosen, New York, 1980.) Now the concept of "substance" which underlies the traditional Catholic theme of Transubstantiation, like the concept of "nature" which underlies traditional Natural Law theory, is a shaft or ray of intellectual light illuminating the world of common experience, providing, in one of its theological applications, a reasonable interpretation of the words: *This is my body, this is my blood*, when these words are given their fullest ontological weight. Yet this *special* mystery of transformation must not be isolated from the *general* transformative presence of the Word made Flesh in the cosmos. As St. Thomas puts it: "the blessing that flowed from the Saviour's baptism, like a spiritual river, filled the course of every stream, and the channel of every spring." (S. Th. 3a, 66. 3 and 4). Much more can this be said of the *earth-baptism* of Christ on Calvary. Protestant eucharistic theology sees the general presence of Christ as specified by the eucharist; Catholic eucharistic theology sees the eucharist as a *special, unique, concrete* presence of Christ in which all else is centred. Here for the (traditionalist) Catholic is marvellous riches, yet it is a wealth of *charity* which is largely lost if it is held divisively or possessively.

this life as passing from Christ to the believer through faith, and at the supersomatic level, so that the bread and wine are seen as sacred symbols merely. At first sight these two eucharistic doctrines and practices seem utterly different and opposed one to the other, yet they are in truth but different ways of entering the great mystery of the prayer of Christ which creates a new world, different ways of announcing his redemptive prayer-unto-death and prayer-beyond-death until he comes in glory. There are also Christian denominations such as the Society of Friends where there is no eucharistic celebration, where, in fact, a direct contact is made with the prayer of Christ, with the continuing reality of Calvary, with the inner fountains of salvation. Because prayer is the centre of valid Christian witness the Quaker approach is essentially valid. It can even be cleansing for us in as much as it says: "your ritual is worthless without the inner sap of prayer that carries the Christ-life along with it, your Real Presence does but accuse you and condemn you unless you respond to its call to sacrificial and serviceable love." To the Quaker we say: "the world is most deeply troubled in the regions of the body which you in a sense leave behind in your prayer, and it is there our liturgy happens; we too lift our eyes to the Kingdom of God but we would take the world along with us."

The Essence of Priesthood

The priest who stands at the altar of God stands in the whole light of the sacrificial prayer of Christ. He stands before the all-holy God and offers himself and his people to this transforming love mediated by the humanity of the ascended

Christ, and of the Woman assumed into the substance of the *ouranos*. The priest, too, in his measure, and at the level of the waiting cosmos, mediates the life and light that flows from the Father, enters within the glow of the triune love of Father, Son and Spirit. The Spirit is present from the beginning, in the very shaping of the new, immaculate conception. But it is only through the ascended humanity of Christ that this marvellous new thing can happen, this descent of the Spirit into the very depths of the cosmos, into that region occupied by the Prince of this World and his legions. The priest stands in the full flowing of this descending power and his whole being is called and challenged by it. Indeed he is ever more conscious that he cannot find the words to express the needs of his people and his own needs, but the Spirit speaks within him with the language of the heart, with cries for which there are no words (Rom. 8:26).

Every man and woman who truly prays shares in the priesthood of Christ, mediates the mystery of the new life and the Kingdom of God and reaches forward towards the Lord's coming in glory. Ordination does not create priesthood, for that is there already in every man and woman who prays with Jesus Christ, whether known by name or not. Ordination, as I see it, does two things: it focuses the priestly reality in a man (or woman) and makes it central and all-pervasive at least *in spe;* secondly it designates a man as the focus of the prayer of the community as a community, and this may be valid and meaningful even though some of those he stands for may well be more prayerful than he.[3]

[3] According to St. Ambrose: "everyone who is anointed into the priesthood (by baptism), is anointed into the kingdom: the spiritual kingdom is also a spiritual priesthood." The "designation" spoken of here is, of course, sacred, sanctifying and sacramental,

Epilogue At Pentecost

As it happens I am writing this chapter at Pentecost in Clermont-Ferrand in central France, having visited a few days ago the village of Sarcenat, and the chateau in which Teilhard de Chardin was born, having also visited Cluny and the new community at Taizé a few miles from Cluny. I wished also to visit Paray-le-Monial but did not manage it, but it has been very much in my consciousness. All these experiences come together in my mind as I try to bring my reflections on Prayer and Priesthood to a conclusion. I think of Teilhard and his *Messe sur le Monde,* and how he came out of this self-enclosed world, and that chateau with its back firmly to the village; came, too, out of this Celtic *massif central* that sees Vercingetorix as France's first hero. I think of Brother Roger of Taizé, and his ecumenical monastery, and the crowds of young people singing and meditating together in the community's vast barn-chapel. I think of the glory that was Cluny, now no more than a museum (for Taizé has ignored Cluny). I think of Margaret Mary of Paray-le-Monial and how she taught the

and can easily be seen, as it in fact *came* to be seen, as impressing a special mark or *character* (in the Greek sense) on the priest. I do not think that Fr. Schillebeeckx in his fascinating study of the priesthood (*Ministry,* SCM Press, Crossroad 1981) takes sufficient account of the presence of the *sacred* in the Christian community, of the way, by a legitimate development, this has been centred and focussed on the priestly ministry. We do not really sanctify the people of God by reducing the sacred to a secular function. Rather is it necessary to affirm that all sacredness, all holiness comes from the Father who alone is utterly holy. (Mk. 10:18). Perhaps I should add that I am not here taking sides on the controversy of the ordination of women, though I am pointing out that women equally belong to that "royal priesthood" spoken of in Peter 2:9. There is a sense in which it can be said that the masculine *rules,* whereas the feminine *is,* the community; yet both energies are present, at least latently, in every man and every woman.

heart of the Catholic world to beat in unison with her own Christ-centered heart. I let these thoughts come and go on this Pentecost Sunday, and I ask myself what lies ahead for the priesthood, for the Church, for the world? I think that somehow a page will soon be turned in man's history, something like a new beginning, perhaps a shaking of the foundations. Perhaps this will come quietly as a new consciousness of love and giving to balance the forces of possessiveness and aggression that are about to destroy us in a nuclear holocaust. Perhaps it will indeed come by way of catastrophe. One thing, however, is clear: only the prayer of Christ can transform the world. That is the challenge which we face as priests, as men designated to pray by the people of God. That is the common glory that shines through all that I have encountered over the past week: Teilhard and Taizé, Cluny and Paray-le-Monial. That was the meaning, the eternal dimension of my First Mass in the Lady Chapel on June 24, 1946. The first Christians, men and women together, waited for the Holy Spirit in a situation of total prayer, *proskarterountes homothumandon en proseuche,* "strongly and constantly united in prayer" (Acts 1:14). As we give him space the same Spirit comes to fill us, and to fill the hearts of the faithful, he who is the source of our prayer and our priesthood.

5

Prayer and the Future

Prayer and the Past

While I was thinking about the title of this chapter and how best I might plough a furrow through such a wide field I happened to visit an ancient burial site called Cairnpapple Hill, and it seemed to me that I should begin here. As one stands here, one thousand feet above the Firth of Forth, one has a wide view of the pasture-land and villages of West Lothian as they open towards the sea and the centres of trade and industry. But the overwhelming vista is that across the valleys of time, across four thousand years to the men who first came here to worship their gods and bury their dead. How completely our little day vanishes into that vast night; how little significance there is in aught we say or do, in aught we feel in this immense desert of vanished significance. What prayer can I say here that is not blown away on the wind, that is not silenced by the voices of the larks that reach back to those ancient ceremonial chants. Surely this prayer of the dead is itself dead; surely history is the graveyard of prayer as of all man's works.

But this is in truth the question. Is prayer subject to time and history, or is it not rather that as Martin Buber says, prayer is not in time, but time (and hence history) is in prayer? Is prayer an activity of mortal man, or rather the activity in which man is more than mortal? When I stand here or at Stonehenge, or at some ancient cloistered shrine covered by the sands of time, or wherever prayer has been established, am I to think of ancient devotion as buried in the ruins, or rather as a light that once lighted never fails? Does my own prayer mingle with the ruins, or make living contact with a reality that does not die?

Prayer is always in the present, in the now that disappears into history, yet all prayer is also in the *presence,* is indeed an affirmation of presence, of man's presence before God, and God's presence to man. The divine presence is not absorbed by history, but rather does this presence absorb history into itself. So it is that, as Plato saw, the impermanence, the "unreality" of temporal events is revealed. But the prayer-event, the prayer-act has an eternal dimension, not only or primarily because it looks to the immortal gods, but because it is a sharing in eternal life, a living contact with that presence which encloses time and history. So it was that when T.S. Eliot in *The Four Quartets* sought for the elusive "point of intersection of the timeless with time" he found it in prayer, and his poem became a call to prayer.

It is by prayer that man enclosed in time reaches outwards and upwards, however gropingly, to a personal centre seen as free of time and decay, upwards, to use Buber's phrase, to the *thou* of his existence. Prayer personalises man and his world, and this sense of personality comes through to us whether we stand on Cairnpapple Hill and recall those ancient folk who placed their dead in this high place and lifted their hands to Chrom or Lugh or whoever, or stand with Eliot among the ruins of Little Gidding where a Christian community gave the whole of life to prayer and worship.

As I stand here on the hill, as Eliot stands by the ancient chapel, it is the human personal centre in each of us that is being touched and challenged, that inner sanctuary where all human dimensions meet: longing, aspiration, fear, celebration, pathos, loneliness, hope, and the rest. All that is felt and known in this sanctuary which is the heart of man reaches down to a finitude that falls into the abyss of nothingness and upwards to the Infinite of Reality and Love. Here is no vision of eye or mind, but the vision of man's own heart, and of the immensity of his need. Yet the vision is always being clarified, and "the shaken mists unsettle", to show something of the *presence,* some glimpse of the face of God.

It is in my present prayer as it reaches in anguish or jubilation in the rich complexity of the human dimension, towards the *thou* of my life, towards presence and fatherhood, that I touch the prayers of the past in the unity of the heart of man. In my prayers I am one with all men and women at all times, past, present, and future. There is no more dolorous or joyful companionship. Neither the archaeologist nor the antiquarian can enter this companionship unless he be a man of prayer, a man of heart, a man of tears. There is indeed a sense in which I desecrate this ancient funeral sanctuary unless when I see it I see it somehow through my tears.

Prayer and the Present

To ask about prayer in the present is to ask about the heart of man in the present, to attempt a finger-on-the-pulse diagnosis of the heart of man. It is at an inner but real level to judge man's breathing, to gauge his temperature, to take stock of his whole state of being, in relation to the Supreme Being that calls him onwards to his own fulness, and beyond that to Its own fulness.

This is a large undertaking, and all that can be attempted here is a very brief sketch. Without any claim to be comprehensive but rather by way of exploration I shall look at some negative factors which reveal themselves as one tries to diagnose the spiritual health of man, to say how it is today with the heart of man as it relates to the heart of God.

The negative factors I wish to look at are: the captive mind, the restless heart, the trapped light, and the coarse vision.

First, *the captive mind.* The mind of man is made for universal truth, for the journey onwards towards ever-widening horizons. Only gradually can the mind find the strength to face this journey; at first it needs a kind of enclosure in the womb of culture and dogmatics. So it is essential to be nurtured in some definite doctrinal system, to be held in the security of ecclesial, social, and political structures. But there must be an open window, a pathway to the far horizons. Otherwise you have the captive mind, which sees its religious commitment in closed inflexible terms, sees it not as a challenge to love and life and communion with all men and all creation, but rather as a kind of package-deal that has to be accepted or rejected, a kind of bullet-proof strait-jacket.

The restless heart, on the other hand, has escaped from captivity, but has not found the way forward to love and life and communion. It has tried this path and that, never persevering on any one path for long, shopping round in our contemporary supermarket of sects and gurus and shiny tins of instant enlightenment. The restless heart is enclosed in its own emotions, is led on by a kind of excitement that cannot face the desert of self-relinquishment, the valleys of patient service, the hills of sacrifice. In the young as they break from the womb of family, culture, or religious fundamentalism, something of this spirit may be necessary, but if it does not somehow face the straight and narrow path, it comes to that state so trenchantly and vividly described in the *Letter of Jude:* "They are clouds carried away by the wind without giving rain, trees that in season bear no fruit."

The trapped light is, as the Americans say, something else again, and I want to delay over it a little. Perhaps I can best describe it by relating a small incident that identifies what is for me a recurring and very sad experience. A few summers ago when I was staying at my mother's house in Killarney there was a knock at the door, and when I opened the door I found a pleasant-looking woman who seemed to radiate a kind of light. I felt a movement of responsive joy as I asked her what I could do for her. It was only a moment, for she began to say that she had come to tell me about the Church of the Latter-day Saints. Then I saw that the light to which I had responded was trapped in a deep well of dogmatism. Not for the first time nor the last, indeed I might say for the thousandth time I found myself looking sadly and helplessly into a well of trapped light, light quite shut in, quite irretrievable, quite beautiful in itself, yet refusing to reach out to the fulness of light or to any other light that might participate in that fulness.

It is only if we really grasp the positive power of all this that we can begin to understand the increasing hold which various sectarian groups have over our young people. There is in every human heart a candle waiting to be lighted. Now this candle can be lighted by any of a thousand or a million candle-lighters; by a retreat master, by a soul-friend, by some guru near or far away, by a Mr. Moon or a Maharaj Ji, by a Mother Teresa, a Billy Graham, or even a Jimmy Jones. You need only look at the picture of an audience listening to Hitler in the Germany of the thirties to see that all these people have received some kind of spark that has lighted up their whole existence. You might feel that these people are really happy, that they have a purpose in life, an inner excitement and vitality. So it was with the thousands of children who were awakened by a preacher and went helter-skelter to death along the road to Jerusalem. Or look at old photographs of the young men of 1914 going off to war, sparked by General Haig or whoever. There is the unforgettable description of the soldiers of the Grand Armée saluting Napoleon as they were swept to their deaths in the icy waters of the Beresina. Or look at the crowds of young people who wait all night to be there in the morning when the ticket office opens to provide magic tickets for the concert of the reigning idol; look at their faces as he sings and capers before them. There is light in their eyes, as there was in the eyes of the children who followed the preacher or the German youth who listened to Hitler, as there is a light in the eyes of this or that sectary you meet in the streets selling Mr. Moon, or David Moses, or "Jesus saves", or whatever.

It would be utterly foolish to think that we are somehow leaving all this behind, that our children's children and their children will not follow the Pied Pipers of their generation. The truth is: the candle is there to be lighted, and somebody will be always at hand to light it. As we move on to the end of a millennium, and a great sense of doom settles over our declining technical era, it is certain that more and more candle-lighters will come forward, and that more and more people will be lightened by them, the young mostly, but sometimes the old as well, as the familiar lights begin to fail in the general decline of our civilization.

The coarse vision takes us to the other end of the spectrum. It owes a good deal to Marxism and Freudianism with their reduction of everything in man to economic or animal terms. It also owes much to the rejection of the father-image in our day, that parricidal approach on the part of many young people towards the values and world of their fathers. It goes with the angry rejection of the way things are, and a cold dismissal of all that was light, joyful, romantic, celebrational, in the world of the fathers. It despises the long labour of learning; it rejects the kind of academic approach to the training of teachers and ministers in which my generation was formed. We must all be out changing the world, helping the poor and oppressed, turning stones into bread.

I am not concerned here with this attitude insofar as it is a hunger and thirst for justice, shared indeed by many of the rejected older generation, but only with a certain kind of vision, a certain kind of aggressiveness in statement, what I can only call a coarseness of perception. It is a refusal to raise the eyes to the hills, or to any of the more spiritual horizons.

Against these four negative factors one must place that radical shift of consciousness becoming gradually apparent among young people today. This change of consciousness takes many forms, and shows itself in phenomena as diverse as alternative communities, on the one hand, and the retrieval of traditional devotions on the other. Its common ground or space, however, is an acceptance of a world or worlds intermediate between matter and pure spirit. All the great religions affirm this intermediate world, and it is everywhere in the New Testament. It is the world of miracles, of the spiritual entities called angels and demons. It is the world of realised symbols, of the blood and water flowing from the side of Christ, of that real vital flow which Paul speaks of when he says Christ lives in him. A misreading of Scripture by the exegetes and theologians has largely translated the clear presence of this world in the New Testament into metaphors and symbols of a purely spiritual reality, whereas what was and is in question is this real supersensible world which is not by any means pure spirit. This is the world of the Resurrection of the Body. It is also the world in which prayer is most immediately powerful and concrete. For though prayer reaches upwards to the pure spiritual Divinity, yet it most of all meets the divine in the world of the spiritual body, what Corbin calls the *Mundus Imaginalis* so carefully distinguished in Sufi mysticism.

I do not want to carry this exploration any further here, my main point being concerned with a shift of consciousness which in some ways counteracts the spiritual diseases with which I have just been concerned. It is true that this consciousness can leave our young people vulnerable to the trapped light and the Pied Pipers who play the tune of cheap enlightenment, but there is nevertheless hope that a deepening of this consciousness may open up a larger world of spiritual presence and presences. In any case this sketchy diagnosis of the present state of the heart of man provides sufficient background for the practical proposal I want to put forward in the final section of this chapter.

Prayer and the Future

I want to bring all I have been saying to a practical head by proposing that the teacher of religion must be in the future a teacher of prayer. I almost said primarily a teacher of prayer, but I do not think there is an order of priority here: the teacher must at all times and at all levels both inform the mind and form the heart. There must be a lived unity of theory and practice, what is sometimes called *praxis,* activity that is ongoing and purposive, part of the vital flow of experience.

In the past, a past that goes back to Cairnpapple and Newgrange and beyond, religion was the pulse of common life; in the more immediate past the individual belonged by the fact of birth and nurture to what T.S. Eliot calls the Christian Commonwealth. In these circumstances the teacher and the pupil belonged together within a *praxis* already established. We find the last remnants of this *praxis* in the school prayers so much resented by some of our contemporaries. Something was being imposed on children which had in fact lost its vitality, and they resented the deadliness of it all. They did not feel within them and around them a vital flow which these prayers expressed and mediated. The living continuity with the Christian centuries and the far reaches of (pagan) religiousness had been lost.

So it is that we can no longer deal in information with an already-given formative power as its background and foundation. So it is that in so many lands religious education is degenerating into a ragbag of comparative religion, elementary psychology, and how to be a good citizen. So it is that the religious education teacher of the future must involve himself in formation at the deepest level of the life-act of the individual pupil. And it is in and through prayer that this individual life-act is grasped as a personal reflection and openness to other persons, and to a personal God.

At this point I am drawing on a remarkable book which appeared in 1967, and made very little impression, though it deserves to rank with Lonergan's *Insight* and Teilhard's *Phenomenom of Man*. The book is *The World of Persons* by a Belgian Jesuit working in Calcutta named Wincklemans de Clety (Burns and Oates, 1967). It has a short foreword by Fr. Copleston, the well-known historian of philosophy, and a most helpful introduction by the Louvain philosopher Jean Landrière. Fr. Wincklemans' method is to analyse human experience in its most general sense and to show that "there is, at the very heart of experience, a central activity, an essential operation which is called life-act." (p. xv). The task of all education and of all ethics is to appropriate or realise reflectively this life-act in its full possibilities, above all to clarify and affirm its utter dependence on the Source of all life, which is God. In this perspective "the implanting of knowledge by the teacher is seen to be formative to the extent to which his own life flows into the lives of his students and their lives into his." (p. 296n).

Fr. Wincklemans does not deal directly with the question of prayer in *The World of Persons;* probably it would come up in a promised theological work which has not, as far as I know, appeared. But, obviously, his description of human growth in self-appropriation and openness to the Source of Life is almost a definition of prayer. One cannot talk in any real sense of the flowing together of the life of the teacher and the lives of his pupils except-insofar as there is a real channel for this flowing, a channel that leads onwards towards the ocean. I see the shaping of this channel as the greatest challenge facing the teaching of religion at all levels in the closing decades of this century.

But this prayer must not be trapped in a dogmatic system, nor can it rest at a superficial level. Precisely because the teaching of religion at the primary and secondary levels must have a strong doctrinal structure, affirmed though not left unquestioned, precisely because of this need of the growing mind, the prayer presence of the teacher must be open and spacious. It must be realised that all men are equal before God, and that all sincere approaches to God must be held in honour.

Yet in its content prayer will draw on doctrine, on Scripture especially. It is amazing what riches can be found in a single text from Scripture especially those used in the Liturgy. But I would plead also for a rediscovery and repristination of those traditional devotions in which Catholicism is so rich. I have been able to share Marian devotion, and the devotion to the Sacred Heart, with some of my Protestant students. Now more than ever the human heart yearns for heart-opening prayers. Now more than ever we need to look to the good spirits, the angels of God who come and go in the Old

Testament and the New. Many Scripture scholars dismiss these beings as mythical, but they give no proof of this beyond the general claim that they do not suit the modern mind. Many of these scholars have not yet caught up with the change of consciousness among the young of which I have spoken. Today angels are definitely *in*, so we might as well take advantage of the turn of the tide. Interestingly the author I have quoted and the Louvain philosopher who writes the preface to the book both accept the central role of "cosmic persons", that is to say, angels.

As I come to an end, my memory goes back to Cairnpapple, and my imagination envisages that inner world which cuts across the flow of time. Time, as Yeats says, moves on, even for the Old Woman of Beara. It moves on towards the end of our millennium as inexorably as the waters move on towards the Falls of Niagara. For many the image is a suitable one, for they see a great catastrophe ahead. Perhaps indeed a page will be turned. But the waters, after much turmoil of froth and spray move on, and so it will be with the river of human life. A thousand years from now, two thousand, I am convinced that there will still be men upon the earth. But I think our sense of the spirit-worlds will have become a kind of perception. Yet one thing will remain as it is, and as it was: the encounter in prayer of the creature with the Source of Life and Love. Prayer encloses the past and the future.

6

The Community of Forgiveness

Terminus

As I sit at my desk this May morning, in "Edinboro town", and wonder how I am going to find an entry into the topic which I have decided to write about, I look out of my window, and see the buses passing along a road about 20 yards away, the buses and the lorries and the cars, though the latter are hidden by a wall; so I am a bit like Plato's cave-dwellers, guessing at the realities behind the appearances. Anyhow, I shall take this red double-decker bus as my first symbol of community. Within it people are going to work, people united by chance and for a short time, people who have never met, all in the capable hands of a man most of them do not even know the name of. They pay as they enter; a ticket pops out; the driver gives them a blank look; they move quickly or slowly to a seat; they sit next to another human being who has a purely spatial existence; they jog along by shops and private houses, by public buildings and parks; they alight and hurry towards office or shop or whatever. They are anybody and everybody; that is what a bus is, an "omnibus", which is the Latin *for everybody*, or was in ancient Rome and medieval Europe. So the slender thread of a broken word binds us all into the far past and the further past.

Take Rome away and the word "bus" disappears, and some other word takes its place. But there are many other threads binding the bus to the past that cannot be taken away. Take away the discovery of the internal combustion engine and the bus won't move; take away the discovery of the wheel and the bus won't roll. So, as I look out of my window at the bus, I am looking back into the far depths of time as well as looking into the life of this city: its shops, offices, factories; and, of course, I can extend this spatial vision as I see some of the passengers alight at Waverley Station, on their way to Glasgow, Aberdeen, London, on their way to ships or aeroplanes, off to the ends of the earth. Moreover, "the ends of the earth" are all with me here, in the tea I am drinking, the paper I write on, the pen, the ink; in the clothes I am wearing, the chair, the desk. Outwards in space, backwards in time, the phenomenon of man extends, supporting me, challenging me, opening me to the dimensions of my own being as everlasting man. Within this human stream, from out of this human earth, I have arisen; and into it I shall soon descend, dust to dust, a part (small or large) of that immense history within which I live and die.

In the bus each person is alone, an isolated unit, alone with her or his thoughts, cares, projects, alone as I am here at my desk, as I open my imagination and feel part of the omnibus of history. I am alone; yet if I reflect for a moment I am part of a mighty community. I am not "just not an island," not simply "part of the mainland." Rather is the whole mainland part of me. Take away part of it, and I fall to pieces. My aloneness is not in my life but in my awareness. As I enter the bus I bring all the generations with me. If one were annihilated I would not be entering the bus. There is a poem by Kathleen Raine which has the title "Seen from the window of a Railway Carriage" in which the poet, as her train passes by the hills of the Scottish Highlands recalls her ancestors' presence among these hills, her ancestors "whose multitude in me clamours for their own".[1] Her awareness dwelt in deep and sometimes terrifying isolation and loneliness — this is clear from her biographical books — yet precisely because of this her poetry is a house of windows opening out on far, even unlimited, vistas of space and time, bringing all people and all things within the glow of her awareness. She is also and primarily a religious poet, as I suppose all good poets are; and all her poems reach towards an affirmation of a Presence that binds all peoples and worlds together. Her poetry is a record of finding community, and finding God in community. Yet, on her own admission, she always has been a very private person, reserved, withdrawn, wrapped into her own world of sensitivity and highly sophisticated expressiveness, not at all the kind of person who would be at home in a community setting. This isolation was her natural place as a poet, as the poet of our common loneliness, the poet of the great community of human loneliness, a loneliness that can run even deeper than the vast solitudes of the hills:

[1] *The Lost Country*, Hamish Hamilton 1971, p. 26.

Into how vast a loneliness we are gathered
Into a strangeness how remote,
Existence without end; presences that yet
Protect us from invading night
And the unbroken silence of the dead.[2]

The mountains, for all their strangeness, offer a kind of protection against the final, inescapable, unendurable strangeness of the inner descent that awaits us all.

But what awaits us at the far end of loneliness? Are we there "alone with the Alone," or simply alone with our uttermost loneliness, a loneliness so deep that annihilation comes as a release and a mercy? It seems to me that the descent is in truth full of company and companionship, strange companions at first that can gradually become familiar. To begin with there are those two dark sisters that reveal themselves at the borders of human companionship, appearing in the twilight as the sun of life's projects and comforting presences goes down. These sisters I name Pathos and Poignancy, companions usually unwelcome yet somehow diffusing mysterious perfumes of fragrance and sweetness. So far are these companions from being alien to man that they are the uniquely special consorts of the human, unavailable to beast or angel. Once we sense their presence in the railway carriage or bus we know that we are in a distinctively and uniquely human world. They are, of course, visible only to the eyes of the heart, but it is the heart that guides us through the desert, that can recognise the companions of our desert pilgrimage. The mystics understand this very clearly. In *The Cloud of*

[2]*Ibid.,* p. 30.

Unknowing it is the "naked intent of the will" that pierces the darkness; in St. John of the Cross, it is the light that burns in the heart (*que en el corazón ardía*) that guides the lover to the beloved. The way of the desert is the way of the heart; and the way of the heart is the way of the desert.

John uses another image of the heart which is relevant here. In the third stanza of *The Living Flame of Love* he speaks of "the deep caverns of sense" which have to become dark and empty in order to be filled with the splendour of "the Lamps of Fire" which are the divine attributes. And he explains that these caverns are immensely vast and deep, because that which is to fill them is, in fact, infinite. The darkness and emptiness which waits for this divine presence is so great and terrible that no man could bear it for long. It is the dark night of the Spirit, the deepest loneliness of the heart, the far reaches of the desert, the place whence the *De Profundis* arises, the time of uttermost testing which every Christian man and woman prays to be spared. Yet this emptying, and darkening is necessary if the divine presence is to find space in the human heart; and some touches at least of this loneliness and darkening and testing must come the way of all who are in any degree open to the presence of God.

This is the way into the blessed community of God's special companions, and in this community God is truly all in all. This is at once Nazareth and Gethsemane, Thabor and Calvary, as we follow the light of Christ "here below"; beyond it is the fulness of life, light, glory, love, the community of the blessed. In his Apocalypse another John strains imagery to breaking point as he describes this community. "Then I saw a new heaven and a new earth, for the first heaven and the first earth had vanished and there was no longer any sea. I saw the holy city, new Jerusalem, coming down out of heaven from God, made ready like a bride adorned for her husband. I heard a loud voice proclaiming from the throne: 'Now at last God has his dwelling place among men. He will dwell among them and they shall be his people, and God himself will be with them!' Then he who sat on the throne said *Behold, I am making all things new*".[3]

I seem to have forgotten all about that morning bus which passed my window as I sat down to write. But in truth, if we believe the Christian message, that is where the bus is going, and in fact it is an *omnibus;* it is for everybody, and we are all companions on this journey. T.S. Eliot in a well-known passage is not talking of a bus but of a train on the London Underground, but the situation is the same, and his words will serve admirably to define it, and to mark the difference between the beginning of the journey and the end.

> When an underground train, in the tube,
> stops too long between stations
> And the conversation rises and slowly fades into
>   silence
> You see behind every face the mental emptiness
>   deepen
> Leaving only the growing terror of nothing to think
>   about.[4]

Here each traveller is enclosed in his own loneliness, as if each were a diver held within a transparent or semi-transparent diving-bell at the bottom of the sea, each doing his

---

[3] *Revelation,* 21 (NEB).
[4] *Four Quartets,* 2.3.

own scrabbling and feeling from time to time the panic of ultimate isolation. At the end, in the final community of love, each diving-bell has dissolved into what is revealed as the ocean of the divine Love, and all loneliness is transcended in the eternal community of love. In this process men and women can help and support each other, can point the way ahead, can even, in some happy community, together provide a kind of first sketch or preshadowing of the final community of love. In this human, time-bound and time-eroded community of love, God is indeed present, is truly to be found, is the hidden sun which illuminates everything.

This final eschatological community of love is a community of complete sharing, complete openness and mutuality, in which my whole being, my whole ego is related to others, is at the service of others, finds the fulness of joy in giving and self-giving. This is the community described in poetic terms by Dante in the later cantos of *Il Paradiso*:

> In that abyss I saw how love held bound
> Into one volume all the leaves whose flight
> Is scattered through the universe around.[5]

It is by no means a fixed, static entranced multitude, but rather a community of continuing action, inter-action, recognition, discovery, companionship. Through the Logos incarnate in Christ through Mary, it creates continuously worlds upon worlds and heavens beyond heavens; it is the place of perpetual light, which is also perpetual life and perpetual living.

[5] *Il Paradiso*, Canto 33, Reynolds translation, Penguin Books 1962.

The Two Communities

This then, is the ideal community in which God is fully found, fully present, in which, in St. Paul's words, "God is all in all."[6] Every human community is a participation in this, and a preparation for this. As a participation in this, every human community is right and true in its direction in so far as it draws forth the harmony and power of the love that illuminates the heavenly community. Because this final community is an ideal more or less hidden in every human heart, we all tend to try to dream of it, to found or to find a community in which this harmony reigns. And at the moments of great common feeling and shared purpose this is achieved. Moreover, every rule or guide followed by a community has as its aim and hope, the achievement of this harmony. That is the one reason why the concept of mutual charity is given priority over everything else. Or perhaps I should say, should be given priority. For there are some communities in which obedience to a rule or a person or a doctrine is given priority over mutual charity. It is, of course, obvious that both attitudes must be present. Abraham Maslow has pointed out that human development operates according to the poles of growth and defence; as we grow we become more vulnerable so there must be mechanisms of defence, chief of which is the security of a rule or an authority to be obediently followed.[7] If these defence structures are too heavy they will kill growth, and so the principle of growth, of

[6] *1 Cor.* 15:28.
[7] See, for example, *Motivation and Personality*, Harper & Row: New York, 2nd Ed. (1970) Ch. 4.

expansiveness and creativity, must also be given its full place. Growth is at once an expression of mutual charity and something made possible by mutual charity. If I truly love my brother, I not only work positively myself, expanding and sharing my deepest being, but I also want to give place and space to my brother to expand. But if I am primarily defensive, I shall not only fail to open out to my brother, to the life around me, I shall also be threatened by my brother's doing so. I shall want him to remain strictly within the limits laid down by the rules, customs, guides, and mentors of the group, as I do myself. Instead of seeing the rule as a marvellous way of shaping true growth, I shall see it as a means of remaining half-dead and keeping my companions in the land of the living-dead.

So we can distinguish two kinds of community, the one open, the other closed; the one a place of growth, the other a place of fossils; the one a place of freedom, the other a place of servitude. I shall call the one messianic, the other, pharisaic. I call the creative, open, community messianic, because it is open to the Christ-presence, the Christ-principle, and the Christ-annointing. The Messiah, the Christ, is the man who has been anointed by the Holy Spirit of God, anointed in order to go forth to a new world, to the fulness of manhood, to the kingdom of God's power and presence. The pharisaic community has put the letter before the spirit, security before eschatological adventure, separation before universal love, obedience to the rule before mutual love. I still remember vividly, the chill I felt in my heart when, on entering the Carmelite Order, I read in the Carmelite Rule, at the very beginning, these words: *totius vitae religiosae basis est obedientia* — the whole basis of religious life is obedience. I have seen the same statement in other religious rules of the pre-Vatican II period. If Vatican II did nothing apart from correcting this it would have been worthwhile. If you read the rule that has emerged as a result of Vatican II, you will find that charity now occupies its true place as the basis of everything, and obedience is kept in *its* place as essential but secondary. In making this change we have simply returned to our origins, as beautifully expressed in the hymn *ubi caritas et amor, Deus ibi est (where* there is love, *there* God is). To the extent, and only to the extent that mutual charity is the atmosphere of the community can it be said that God is present in it. Neither achievement (in education, social work, art, or philosophy) nor liturgy and worship, nor the bringing in of a new age can take the place of mutual charity. Indeed St. Paul goes so far as to say that not even martyrdom, nor the working of miracles, nor preaching the Good News of salvation, can avail anything if charity is missing.[8] It is by charity alone that a community as a community may be said to find God, to participate in the final community in which God is all in all.

Yet there is one matter in which the wayfarer community differs radically from the blessed community, that of forgiveness and reconciliation. In the wayfarer community charity shows itself most crucially as forgiveness, and as the acceptance of forgiveness. It is in forgiveness above all that God is present in the community, that the wayfarer community is truly messianic. It is in the absence of forgiveness, given and received, that a wayfarer community is a pharisaic community. In order to explain what I mean and perhaps establish its reasonableness, I must ask you to look closely at forgiveness as one of the primary dimensions of man's being and becoming.

[8] *1 Cor.* 13:1-3.

Forgivingness

It is sometimes hard to forgive; it is almost always hard to be forgiven. Readiness to forgive is one of the signs of final maturity, that entry into adulthood which usually comes in the early twenties, though it has its foreshadowing from quite an early age. Readiness to be forgive comes much later, and is one of the signs of that second maturity which usually comes in the middle forties. I want to explain these seemingly dogmatic assertions more fully, and perhaps show that they are reasonable assertions.

But first let me try to put aside some erroneous or incomplete notions of forgiveness. If somebody steals my watch and I continue to treat him as an honest man, that is not forgiveness, but a kind of falsehood and foolishness. If somebody steals my watch and I say, as Voltaire did, that being a petty thief is much less criminal than the way of the generality of men, that is not forgiveness, but a kind of cynicism based on a half-truth. If a man steals my watch, and I simply forget that he has done so and continue to treat him as a trusty friend, that is a kind of magnificent absentmindedness, an attitude that may indeed be admirable in its largeness and detachment; but it is not forgiveness. If somebody wrongs me, and wounds me, and I decide that I am too good a Christian or too noble a character to take any notice of such things, I am, again, rather admirable, but I am not really forgiving the man who has done me wrong. This question of one's self-image is indeed very subtle: to have an image of myself as the sort of man who always forgives may well prevent me from ever being truly forgiving. What I am doing in this case is using my neighbour as a rag to polish the brass of my self-esteem.

What then is forgiveness? It is, to begin with, something personal; it involves a person-to-person encounter with my neighbour. Further, it is founded on truth and sincerity: if I am robbed by A, then A has robbed me; if I have been insulted by B, B has insulted me. If I try to push the truth away, it will find its own way back, piercing through the wall of my insincerity. Finally, forgiveness is an exercise of love: it is an affirmation of the bond that unites me to my neighbour, of my participation in his life, of my readiness to suffer for him, in him and with him. "Love," says St. Paul, "does not take offence, keeps no score of wrongs". In other words, forgiveness comes when I enter into the precincts of love within my heart.

Forgiveness then, is personal, truthful, loving: these are its conditions, indicators of where within the great "caverns of sense" it can be found. But these indicators do not yet identify the special light, the characteristic aroma, the air, the atmosphere, of the forgiving heart. The place of forgiveness is very deep, very far in within the country of the heart. It is a valley situated beyond the mountains of acceptance, beyond the dark valleys of sorrow, the flowering valleys of peace, beyond the wells of joy, and the wide seas of pathos. It may be compared to a pleasant green upland lying under the sunshine of love, yet forever traversed by the shadows of clouds that pass across the sky, forever watered by rain that is sometimes "the flail of the lashing hail," sometimes touched by the frolic winds of playfulness, always freshened by the dews of night and the fresh wind of morning. This is just a kind of dance of images; but those who have lived in a real living community will, I think, accept the images as true to the experience of forgiving, though I should also have put in an image to stand for celebration, for this can, at times, be a song in the heart as the hail and heavy clouds pass over and the sun comes out again.

What I am saying is that forgiveness is not simply an action or type of action, something we do or do not do, something put upon us as a kind of task and test. Rather is it an inner dimension to be discovered and explored. And my shower of metaphors was trying to express its relationship to other human dimensions such as pathos, sorrow, playfulness and the rest.[9]

Some years ago an article entitled "God and Forgiveness" appeared in the Scottish journal *The Philosophical Quarterly*.[10] It was written by a Canadian academic named Anne Minas, and it proved quite clearly and conclusively that God cannot really be said to forgive, for God being invulnerable and omniscient can neither be injured in any way, nor can he change his mind about any supposed wrong or injury done to himself or anybody else. Dr. Minas took up the various meanings of "forgive" and "forgiveness" set down in the Oxford English Dictionary and showed that in none of these senses could forgiveness be attributed to God. The article is entirely convincing within its own terms; and it does illuminate a common imprecision of thought and language. But neither the O.E.D. nor Dr. Minas really touch forgiveness as a basic human dimension in which the human mirrors, however dimly and darkly, one of those "lamps of fire" which are the attributes of God.

I have spoken of the celebration of forgiveness, the deep joy it can bring, and all I have to say rests for its acceptance on a

---

[9]See *Heaven in Ordinarie*, Ch. 1.
[10]Vol. 25, No. 98 (Jan 1975).

shared experience of this joy. Like all deep and pure joy this joy is bound up with creativity. It is the joy of new being, of a new world, the joy of harmony momentarily glimpsed as it proceeds from our action and attitude. Forgiveness creates; the readiness to forgive is the expression of creative love. It may involve pangs, pains, like childbirth or artistic creation; it may even involve a kind of breaking up or refining of the material to hand. Forgiveness is not soft and easy; it may be a refining fire. I do not forgive the young man who broke into my flat some months ago by letting him go scot-free. The prayer I send towards him reaches down into his depths, breaking through the outer layers of self-indulgence and hypocrisy. What is vitally important is that I am not indifferent to him, to his real needs, to the spirit within him that seeks aid and light. I may decide that one way into this is to invoke the judiciary process of the community to which we both belong, though I may well feel that these processes are defective. I may see him more clearly by looking into his background, but I am not in the business of seeking excuses for him. My forgiveness can only work through the truth of the situation, just as creative artists can work only by seeing or trying to see materials as they are.

Forgiveness then, is an expression of creative love, a reflection in the human of the central divine attributes of love and creative power. It is connected with other human dimensions such as sorrow, joy, pathos, playfulness, belonging. Like all human dimensions it is the meeting of finite and the infinite in man. The discovery of forgiveness is part of the achievement of first or basic maturity. The road towards forgiveness is the road of prayer; it receives a new depth and clarity with the coming of mystical prayer. It is an aspect of that anointing of the spirit which creates a messianic community.

Forgiveness may be called the cement which keeps a community together. If it is lacking, the units fall back into themselves; structures harden into pharisaism; a false peace, a false harmony is achieved by what may be called the skill of sophisticated avoidance; corns seldom trodden on are allowed to grow freely until you have a community of cripples. "Bless us O Lord, as we hobble along towards the kingdom of heaven." Where nobody really encounters anybody else, there is no need for forgiveness.

One very subtle form of avoidance is by way of a kind of self-imposed sweetness and light. I mean the community imposes it on itself. I was talking recently to a young woman whose sister has joined a religious sisterhood, a Catholic congregation, all regular and above board, not one of those sects that destroy all growth by definition, so to speak. The young woman said that her sister's letters had become quite unreal, nothing but ,pious twaddle and twitterings. She wanted me to tell her, if I could, whether her sister would ever become real again. I had to say that I had seen women live their whole life in this kind of cuckoo-clock cloister world, that all she could do was to keep up her own sense of reality, that there was some hope of a change for the better at the time when her sister awakened to the wide cracks underneath the surface harmony, when she would have to choose between conflict and connivance, between the way of true forgiveness and the way of total avoidance. One thing I was sure of: the sister outside the cloister was nearer to "the wild imaginative God" than the sister in the dove-cotes.

I have spoken of forgiveness as the cement that keeps the community together, but I do not want to press this image too far. Indeed a better image would be air, fresh and full of light.

Forgiveness it is that keeps the atmosphere of a community fresh and invigorating. And at times it seems to bring out a fragrance that can almost be felt and breathed in, like the breathing of Christ as he said farewell to his disciples.

Yet forgiveness rests on truth, as has been said; and sometimes the truth is sharp and may appear cruel. The young man who burgled my flat does not "get away with it." It is only if I treat him impersonally and indifferently that I am ready to let him get away with it. If I truly accept him, then I must reach down to the truth buried deep down in him beneath the heavy layers of pretence and selfishness. In this reaching down, in this penetration towards the truth, my anger may well provide the energy I need; so my anger may well be very precious. It must not be crushed down nor yet dissipated intemperately, rather must it be tempered into a sharp knife which is there to cut deep, and so on to serve him. If he does not come, another may come. The knife becomes then part of the armoury of forgiveness which is an essential part of my being with others and my belonging with others.

On the other hand I do not "get away with" anything if I live in a community of truth and true forgiveness. My pretences, weaknesses, pomposities, ambivalences, are pierced, prodded, and exposed, by those who truly love me. This is not a comfortable life, but neither was living with Jesus of Nazareth a comfortable life. Yet it has the great and unique comfort of absolute acceptance, of a love that will not fail. In the togetherness of community, as in the togetherness of friendship, there is only one sin, one betrayal, that of going away, of withdrawing, of exclusion. I mean definitively and in the deep heart's core, for of course there are people and circumstances in relation to which we can act truly and lovingly only by a kind of tactical withdrawal, when the heart has to wait, perhaps for many years. To the outside observer this may look like exclusion and unlovingness, may look like unforgivingness; but it is in fact the opposite, being the only possible way towards a hoped-for future real relationship. In this connection I feel that the famous text about leaving one's gift before the altar and going first to be reconciled to one's brother has sometimes been misunderstood, as if I had to connive with my brother's selfishness and foolishness, and become reconciled at all costs.[11] Reconciliation is real only in the atmosphere of truth, and has to await this atmosphere: the time for that may not yet have come, and anything I do now may but serve to deepen the fog of unreality. Forgiveness faces into reality not away from it.

Forgiveness

Yet for the forgiven, reality may not be easy to face. Let us suppose that for my young burglar the reality reveals a basic option for selfishness, a world-sense entirely filled by an ego-sense. In forgiving him I do not accept this. I show him to himself as he is; and in doing this I show him that in his will, in his deepest being, he destroys the earth, the heavens, destroys me, destroys himself. If I am to forgive for the injury done to me, to himself, to the whole of creation, I must at all costs, reach down into a deeper layer of his being, where he is open to truth, to reality, to love. If I am to do this, he must help me, he must, like the Prodigal, return to his true self; he must, from

[11] *Matthew* 5:23.

out of his freedom, break through the circle of his selfishness. He must undergo a "change of heart" (*metanoia*) before forgiveness has any meaning. There is no other way into the kingdom of truth and love. There is no other way to prepare for the coming of Christ and the Messianic world. There is no other way of entering the messianic community. Christ cannot come unless there is first a man sent from God who says: repent; change your ways; do penance. This is the way of true forgiveness; and there is no other way. Apart from that, there are the various forms of pseudo-forgiveness, such as "being let off," being treated as a puppet, being accepted into a Fagin world where we are all crooks together. All these leave the evil doer where he is; forgiveness cuts to the bone.

So it is, that people avoid forgiveness and seek connivance. So it is that the Pharisee protects himself from forgiveness by means of a cloud of self-delusion. So it is that the pharisaic community is held together by mutual connivance, as the messianic community is held together by mutual forgiveness, given and received. It is fascinating, terrifying even, to watch the spirit of connivance take over in a group or community, how a kind of heaviness descends as people's hearts close up, how spontaneity becomes brisk, and briskness becomes perfunctory, and perfunctoriness takes the place of love.

In all this the individual is avoiding the light, the light that would shine into the depths and reveal what is there and what is not there. There are a thousand ways of hiding from the light within a community: by role-playing, by jocoseness heavy or light, by emitting a murky aura of captious complaining and criticism. To begin to open to the light is to begin to live in one's own truth, to stop playing games, to speak one's mind, and so draw the fire of others' mind-speaking. It is to become vulnerable both to love and to hate; it is to lay oneself open to radical rejection or acceptance. It is in a very special way to see God in the neighbour, opening to God's judgement in the neighbour's vision of me, seeking an ever greater clarity and sensitivity in this vision as it comes nearer to the Divine. Thus the only way of escape from misunderstanding and rejection is *into* the light. To be fully forgiven is to be fully exposed, fully known, brought under the light of total acceptance and total love.

In a recent article, the Benedictine theologian, Dom Sebastian Moore undertakes a penetrating analysis of the roots of forgiveness; and he puts forward the thesis that we all have a radical need for forgiveness because we carry with us a load of what he calls "generic guilt." This we incur as we leave the "psychic womb," the community into which we were born, which encloses, supports, and sustains us. We are guilty because we have been chosen to be our own individual selves; and we use this guilt as a cloak against the full encounter with freedom. He who would take this guilt away takes away our false security; so we must reject or destroy him in order to protect ourselves.[12]

I do not think I could go all the way with Dom Sebastian when he says that Christ is the one who by taking our guilt on himself, shows us that in fact we are not guilty. I would say rather that the light of Christ reveals all the real and destructive dark energy within man, as well as showing how truly he has covered over his true self and his true freedom. The forgiveness of Christ is the bringing forth of that deeper self

[12]Christian Self Discovery in *Lonergan Workshop* 1 (Ed. by F. Lawrence), Scholars Press, Missoula Mountains, U.S.A., 1979.

where our true freedom dwells. To accept this forgiveness is to cast away all masks and pretences, and to walk free and entirely vulnerable both to the light of Christ and the menacing darkness of the world. To accept forgiveness is to accept my deepest truth and my deepest freedom. But this truth is that of myself I am absolutely nothing; my deepest freedom is the freedom to be loved, to be, as it were, at the mercy of those who love me.

Here we touch on the root of most of our personal "hang-ups" and neuroses, the inability to be loved, which shows itself in all kinds of odd and unexpected ways, for instance, in a kind of "daring the lover," making myself deliberately objectionable in order to show that the lover does not really love me. Forgiving may here be very difficult indeed, but even at this, the being forgiven is even more difficult. Most of us have had, at some time this experience, actively or passively.

Both ways this can be the greatest challenge of community living. The paradox is that it is only in so far as we learn to be forgiven that we can thus radically forgive; and conversely, it is only when we learn radical forgiving that we can open ourselves to the light of radical forgiveness that bears not on this or that offence or ugliness of behaviour but rather on our innermost secret self, as needing acceptance in its very being.

To be accepted is to take the risk of not being accepted; to be loved is to be at the mercy of the beloved; for love is free, and what is freely given can be freely taken away. The only security in being loved is absolute trust, a trust that is at once trust in oneself, and in him who loves me, and in God. This is a great and precious thing, this radical trust; and every true community is a school of trust. Within it mutual trust is developed, tested, purified, shaken and sifted. This can mean conflict, hurt, and at times, a kind of confusion and despair. But if there is basic goodwill then peace will always prevail, reconciliation will always come. In the first messianic community there was much disruption, much disagreement, even anger at times (as between Peter and Paul), but through it all the Christ-love prevailed. It is only when a community becomes wise in its own conceit, superior, and self-righteous, that it begins to lose that messianic simplicity and unction, that child-like openness to God and the future, and that it oppresses and saddens the Holy Spirit of God.

The Final Destination

I have tried to show that every true community, every community in which God truly dwells, and is truly found, is a community of forgiveness.[13] In such a community, God is always awakening anew, both in the community and in the persons who compose it. St. John of the Cross has a wonderful passage in *The Living Flame of Love* on the awakenings of God in the soul, which he sees as in truth the awakening of the soul to God, though it seems, and very vividly seems, as if the Holy Spirit of God had awakened within the spirit. As an image of this awakening at its fullest he uses that of a garden of aromatic plants and flowers when all the perfumes of the garden are

[13]When I had written this paper, I came on a "working paper" on "Discovering Community" by Rosemary Haughton, and find that she too, from a somewhat different viewpoint, sees forgiveness as central to community. She writes: "Repentance is the foundation of true community. To repent, to return to the Lord, means to rediscover the values of human life, the presence of God as the place where we touch each other, a presence we mediate. The experience makes stringent demands. It is a fierce discipline but a manifestly liberating one."

shaken together. Perhaps these deep awakenings are beyond us, or far ahead of us on the road, yet we too, each in our own way and measure, can partake of these awakenings. This experience will come if we try to enter deeply into the community of forgiveness. It is the way to peace, even though it is not always a peaceful way.

As I finish writing these thoughts I am again sitting at my window in the early morning watching the traffic in its first fervour, so to speak. I have not seen any bus passing, as it is not yet six-o clock; but soon they will be passing by, heavy with human concerns, with human pains, excitements and aspirations. People are together whether they wish it or not. The world is for everybody, *pro omnibus*. Every bus has its destination on its forehead; but more truly all buses have the one destination, and the one destination is *Nowhere* or *Somewhere*. I read it as *Somewhere*; and that place is always en route for the final destination, where God will be all in all, *in omnibus and pro omnibus*. As the grey morning lightens here "in Edinboro town" my thought runs out over this round earth, with its circling moon, and the great light of the sun far away. If that sun were to fail for one moment we should not only be plunged into darkness, but lost in the cold immensity of space. Yet another sun shines within the heart. I can hide from this sun of God's love, or I can open wide to it. As I open to it, I see all those around me in this new light, and I salute them in the sharing of this light. No longer am I troubled by the cold dark immensities of physical space: this is but the outside of the great omnibus of creation. Within, the forgiven heart fills all the space of the universe of harmonious spirits. In finding his own heart man finds the whole universe and shares it with everybody.

7

The Fourth Liberation
Self-Relinquishment in the
Cloud of Unknowing
and the *Epistle of Privy Counsel*

The Four Liberations

All the Christian mystics have much to say on self-abandonment and self-relinquishment as part of the process of that union with God which is the goal and fulfilment of the whole contemplative enterprise. At first sight the two terms seem to refer to the one thing, and indeed they are by certain authors used interchangeably; yet they can be seen as quite distinct processes, as quite distinct stages in the interior journey. Self-abandonment is a kind of "letting-go" into the divine source and homeland of man's being. St. Thérèse of Lisieux calls it "the way of spiritual childhood," in which the faithful soul sees God as a loving father, and takes refuge in the arms of his encompassing love. It is an attitude clearly commended in the New Testament in texts such as that which tells us to "consider the lilies of the field." One of the most celebrated books on the subject is De Caussade's *Self-Abandonment to Divine Providence;* as its title indicates this book explores the implications of a complete "letting-go" into the mysteriously demanding and supporting lovingness of the Heavenly Father's care. It is something gentle and flowing, rather like falling asleep; for in falling asleep we mysteriously let go into what is deeply sensed as an alternative mode of life and being. It is a handing over of oneself as a child to its mother: secure, trusting, joyful. It is complete to the extent that the Heavenly Father counts for everything, that the heart is not set and centred on "the things of earth," on personal possessing or the possessing of persons. In its fulness this state lies far along the spiritual path. Yet it is in itself simple, easy, delightful. It is the primary *Abba* of glory and delight.

Self-relinquishment is quite another matter, though it too is a stage, perhaps the final stage, of the spiritual journey. It is of all spiritual experience the most bitter and the most terrifying. It is perhaps "the test" which shows itself at the end of the Abba prayer of Jesus: "put us not to the test." Yet it is also the great and final liberation of the human spirit, the culmination of a long process of liberation wherein we can distinguish four stages or moments.

The first liberation concerns the world of the senses, what variously holds man captive within his bodily being: attachment to food and drink, physical *eros,* all that joy and pride of life rising in its own order to the charms and blandishments of sight and sound and the delicate sensitivities of "educated" taste and touch. This world has its own place obviously, its own beauty, its own sophistication. But when it defines the limits of man's world it becomes a prison, and the "spirit" yearns to be free, if only to have real joy in the things of this same world of the senses. For most people this liberation involves *ascesis,* a programme of taming and trimming, of denial and a kind of death, the active "dark night" of sense, to use the language of St. John of the Cross. And this process may take years. In a real sense it has to continue as long as life lasts, though it has a very different quality and import before and after the first liberation. This liberation comes both gradually and suddenly, gradually inasmuch as it is a preparation for the mystical, suddenly inasmuch as it is the first fruits of the mystical. The ascetical brings control like that of a rider who has brought his horse under his mastery; the mystical it is that transforms this control into that spontaneity where horse and rider are one. The metaphor of the horse is worth keeping in mind—it goes back to Plato in fact—as it is the basic energy thus tamed and "harmonised" that carries a man through all the hardships and terrors of the further journey. Put it this way: there may be times when the rider gets off and walks or coaxes the horse forward through narrow places, yet unless he has the horse to bear him up most of the time he will not travel far or fast.

The second liberation has to do with possession and possessions. It is this especially that we find emphasised in the teaching of Jesus. In a sense it includes the first liberation, for it is only the man who is free of the hold of sensual desires and passions who can disentangle himself from possessions. But possession also means power, having a "place in the sun" being "somebody," looking for honour and prestige, and all this cuts very deep. In a characteristic paragraph Teresa of Avila asks why men, so much more "learned" than women, so seldom arrive at the mystical level; and she answers that it is because they are so full of their own good name, their *honra*, the desire to be respected by other men. This is of course a servitude, and it is very hard to break. That is why "humiliation," the practice of humility, has been so much held in honour in the monastic tradition. Of course *honra* is very subtle in finding a place for itself, and sustenance, and it can grow fat on the dry bread of humiliation if needs be. ("See I am not only modest and humble, but I don't even notice such things. I am just very ordinary, but please don't admire me for this.")

Obviously one can give up external possessions in one dramatic Franciscan act, but this other dispossession can only come in deep darkness, through great tribulation and "over-turnings," at the far edge of the desert. In its fulness it can come only as part of the mystical gift, through the purifying light and fire of the transforming Spirit.

There is another kind of possessiveness which can go very deep, which for people otherwise generous and open can go deepest of all: the possession of persons. This includes the whole domain of attachment to parents and relatives, of "falling in love," of being "held" by the image of some attractive personality. Perhaps the word "holding" expresses best this kind of servitude. One is held by the other's image, as one tries to hold and possess the other's being. Few escape this servitude; indeed it seems to be a normal stage in the spirit's development. It can occur many times; it can strike in youth, maturity, old age. It can be overt or hidden, openly erotic, or only latently so. It can be disreputable, or it can be safely situated within a respectable framework, as in, for instance, the case of the possessive husband or wife, the possessive mother or father. It takes a thousand forms but they all have one thing in common: the possessive heart and the "holding-ness" which this involves. It must be carefully distinguished from true friendship, true love, which opens out to life, to others, to the divine presence, which is not without tears but *is* without bitterness, wherein loss and bereavement is a flowing and a freeing for all its sorrow.

For many of the mystics this second liberation has been dramatic and traumatic, a breaking of the heart from which, after a while or almost immediately, a deeper lovingness issued forth. In some traditions there is talk of the divine "favours," the first favours connected with the first liberation, the second with this second liberation, coming at the far side of a great desert of desolation and "letting-go." Indeed the spiritual journey in its early stages especially, but in a way all through, is seen as a succession of dark and bright, expansion and constriction, desert and flowering meadows. Usually the second liberation is followed by a long period of sweetness and light, the deepening and consolidation of an inner radiance which is the ambience of spiritual love and friendship. There are plenty of trials and disappointments, but the inner light that shines beyond the second liberation is never lost, though it may operate at different psychic levels, some of which are below the level of direct consciousness.

This is a secure and happy life for all its hardships; and it would seem that there are some who never get beyond it. This is, so to speak, right for them; though it must be said that there is danger that they may become monotonous and predictable in what they do and say, losing that openness to the future and the radical unknown which is the mark of spiritual childhood. There is indeed a deeper sense in which the only "right" way or state is forward to complete freedom. For there are still liberations to achieve before full freedom is achieved.

The third liberation may be called liberation from dogma. This does not mean that dogma is either despised or rejected any more than the things of the body and the heart are despised or rejected in the first two liberations. Here too what is transcended had and has its essential role, but the had and the has are deeply different things though apparently the same. It is one thing to live in a house and never leave it; it is quite another to live in a house as the home to which one returns. In the first case one lives in a closed world; in the second case one lives in an open world with all its challenges, dangers, insecurities, surprises, adventures. All the more truly because of this wide freedom is the place of return invested with that "home-light" that is one of the wonders of the heart of man. Yet the spirit does travel far by strange paths into strange places. It is the open sea with all its hazards and terrors. How simple and beautiful and alluring they can seem then, the secure doors and well-fastened windows of home with all their comforting presences, and at first it seems that within the wide enclosure of this demesne—for it is a house set in spacious grounds— can be found all that the mystical life demands, that in truth it can be lived here best of all. So it is that the mystical pilgrim discovers with joy that marvellous corner where the mystical treasures are kept, an obscure corner certainly but, nevertheless, an accepted part of the household of the faith. He does not pause to ask himself why something so uniquely precious should be thus hidden away, and even treated with a certain suspiciousness. If he did but think more on this, he might the sooner see that the mystical is not entirely at home in the household of the faith.

But if he moves on this is made clear to him in other ways. He will find two things happening. In the first place, he will come under suspicion by the orthodox, and be seen as an "outsider": this will appear in all sorts of ways, some very subtle, some not at all subtle. In the second place, he will come to question some of the basic tenets of orthodoxy, all those tenets in fact which seem to limit the goodness and love of the Being who is drawing him on. "The drawing of this love and the voice of this calling" begins to centre all his theology around itself. He is being forced outwards, into the unknown. A new desert has to be traversed, a desert even more daunting than the desert of the senses leading to the first liberation, and the desert of the heart leading to the second liberation. In the first two deserts he knew whither he was bound, and could see the way ahead however arid it looked, however beset with dangers; here the way is without signposts or clear landmarks. All is ambiguity, and the bones of the dead are all around, the bones of those who have struck forth boldly and come more or less spectacularly to grief, sometimes bringing others to grief as well. Or at least, so the story is told by the scribes within the household. Perhaps the bones are but a cautionary tale, not real bones at all. Yet some of these bones seem real enough, and the falsity of the prophet or messiah seems beyond question. But all is ambiguity in this way; all is at once a challenge to courage and calling up of fear. It is the world of the *Cloud of Unknowing*, for the cloud not only hides the face of God; it also hides the face of theology, of dogmatic security.

There is much that could be said about the varieties, degrees, moments, and paradoxes, of this liberation. But I am here concerned primarily with the fourth liberation, and so I must press on. But one thing must be said to forestall, at least partially, misunderstanding. It is that the liberation from dogma has nothing to do with indifferentism or even with liberalism, where liberalism means non-concern with religious issues or non-commitment to religious principles. The liberated mystic respects dogma as he respects the world of the heart and the world of the senses, but he is in no way limited or constrained by dogma, nor does he locate the divine presence exclusively within his own religious family or denomination. Yet is is here that (normally) his spirit is at home, and so he treats everything within it with respect. Everything, even the least observance or tradition. So it was that Teresa of Avila could say that she would die for the least observance, as she also said that she wanted it to be known that she died "a daughter of the Church." These statements are sometimes completely misunderstood by some of her dogmatical followers. These are not sectarian statements: Teresa died a true daughter of the church because she had very painfully achieved full independent maturity of spirit.

And so we come to the fourth and final liberation, variously described or only hinted at by the great mystics, touched on now and then by other sensitive people, obscurely encountered in the despairs and annihilations of certain types of depression. I am concerned here with one special statement of this liberation, that presented in the 14th century *Cloud of Unknowing* and its sister treatise *The Epistle of Privy Counsel.* I shall look especially at chapters 43 and 44 of the *Cloud* and Ch. 8 of the *Epistle.* But first it may be well to say what is the main theme and emphasis of these writings.[1]

---

[1] The standard edition of these books is that of Phyllis Hodgson in the Early English Text Society series, Oxford University Press 1944. The most easily available edition is that

The Two Clouds

The *Cloud* is the main statement of the author's theme and the *Epistle* is mostly concerned with clarifying several points which, it would seem, the recipient of the first writing found obscure or hard to accept. Further reflection and the fact that he has already unburdened himself of his main message, gives the author a kind of lightness of touch and freedom of expression in the *Epistle* which sometimes gives an impression of poetry rather than prose: it is a kind of celebration of the mysteries of mystical union with God. But it is the one statement that is being made in both: that the highest work of the spirit of man is a blind stirring or "intent" of love focussed on God hidden in a cloud of "unknowing." All else leads round to this insight, or explains it, or derives from it. "Lift up thine heart unto God'with a meek stirring of love; and mean himself and none of his goods. And there to look that thou loathe to think on aught but himself, so that nought work in thy mind nor in thy will but only himself. Cease not but travail therein till thou feel list. For at the first time when thou dost it, thou findest but a darkness, and as it were a cloud of unknowing, thou knowest not what, saving that thou feelest in thy will a naked intent unto God. This darkness and this cloud, howsoever thou dost, is betwixt thee and thy God, and hindereth thee, so that thou mayest neither see him clearly by

in the Penguin Classics, edited by Clifton Watters. This edition is clear and readable, but at a very high price in dignity and force of diction. The flavour of the original is largely preserved in another available edition, that of Abbot Justin McCann, first published by Burns & Oates and now available from Anthony Clarke Books of Wheathampstead, Hertfordshire, England. In this article I follow the McCann edition using also the Hodgson standard edition.

light of understanding in thy reason, nor feel him in sweetness of love in thine affection. And therefore shape thee to hide in this darkness as long as thou mayest, evermore crying after him whom thou lovest. For if ever thou shalt see him or feel him, as it may be here, it must always be in this cloud and in this darkness" (*Cloud* Ch. 3)

The relationship of this approach to God, with that of Pseudo-Denis—Denis "Hid-Divinity" as he was called at this time—would be obvious even if the author had not acknowledged this influence. But, of course, the author does acknowledge this influence. In chapter 70 he tells us: "Truly whoso will look in Denis's books, he will find that his words will clearly confirm all that I have said or shall say, from the beginning of this treatise to the end." For the author of the *Cloud* and his contemporaries Denis was the *Areopagite*, the Athenian disciple of St. Paul, and his writings were regarded as quasi-canonical. He was, it seems a disciple of Proclus, and through him a whole stream of Neo-platonism flowed into Christian mystical theology. In this tradition God is the ineffable one beyond the worlds of Soul and Spirit, beyond the world accessible to the human spirit as cognitive. Any effort to conceptualise the divinity, to understand or apprehend it, could serve to falsify it, reducing it to terms of Soul or Spirit. Yet is is true that Spirit and Soul are emanations of the One in the marvellous hierarchy of creation, and so there is a way, an approach to the One. Indeed this approach is an essential part of the journey. Only he who has explored the limits of the created world can truly open to the sublime darkness beyond these limits. Here as elsewhere there is no greater mistake than that of confusing the "darkness" of mystical knowledge with ordinary ignorance or intellectual torpor. The author of the

Cloud puts this in his own way by saying that this "work" is something available only to those entering on the highest stage of the spiritual journey, beyond the *Common* stage, beyond the *Special* stage in which a man gives himself spiritually and fully to God's service, beyond the *Singular* stage which is the way of mystical illumination (*Cloud* ch. 1). It is the way of the *Perfect*, that is to say, of those who have followed the light until it has led them on to the threshold of this darkness. The "unknowing" in question is in no way a substitute for "knowing," for the labours of learning and the joys of insight: rather is it an unknowing *beyond* knowing, an opening to the One beyond all being and all knowing of being.

But it does mean a going beyond and a leaving behind. In order to face forward into the cloud of unknowing the spiritual pilgrim must constantly relinquish all else, all goods and all knowing, "putting a cloud of forgetting between himself and all creatures that ever be made." (*Cloud* ch. 5). These two clouds are very different, being in a sense contraries: the one above, the other below; the one encountered by man, the other made by man; the one in the order of knowing, the other in the order of seeking. This last difference is important. The tradition to which the *Cloud* belongs is as has been said strongly Neoplatonic, and therefore may be said to spurn the earth and the whole world of the perishable body. But it is also a Christian tradition, and therefore incarnational and sacramental, emphasising not so much rejection and forgetfulness of the material world as detachment from that world. Yet from the beginning the Christian Gospel was preached not to an elite, but to "the poor," to Everyman; it brought a message of redemption rather than transcendence. The Son of Man came eating and drinking, and weeping too, and rejoicing: he was after all the Son of *Man*. In this tradition the world is rejected and transcended inasmuch as it is the world of possessions and possessiveness, but it is, all the same, *sacrament,* the place of redemption, itself involved in the process of redemption. In a sense, nothing is forgotten; all is subsumed, taken along, made to live again in the world of the Resurrection. So the cloud of forgetting is a letting go of the things of earth, a liberation from them, but it is not a true forgetting of them: they are still precious but now they are in their place, seen contemplatively and not possessively.

This tradition of acceptance with detachment is one of the strands of the *Cloud* and the *Epistle,* always there, but sometimes hidden in the twist of the argument by the other Neoplatonic strand which affirms a total forgetting of earthly things.

This then is the central affirmation of the *Cloud:* a total seeking of God in intellectual darkness with a naked intent of the will ever striving to pierce this darkness (the "cloud"), and a relinquishment of all this in a cloud of forgetting. It is against this background that the author treats of what I have called the fourth and final liberation of man's spirit.

The Final Liberation

"Thou shalt find, when thou has forgotten all other creatures and all their works—yea! and also all thine own works—that there shall remain yet after, betwixt thee and thy God, a naked knowing and a feeling of thine own being: this knowing and feeling must always be destroyed." (*Cloud,* ch. 43). Here there is question of a culmination, something that can only come at the end of a long process.

This process, I would contend, is reasonably described in the three stages of liberation, though the author of the *Cloud* does not use this language but speaks rather of the cloud of forgetting. It is clear in any case that the cloud of forgetting is not a simple phenomenon but has degrees and moments: all creatures, all their works, all "thine own works" are the matter of separable achievements of "forgetting." "All thine own works" may well be equivalent to what St. John of the Cross calls "spiritual goods," and may well extend to one's own intellectual lights and theological erudition, as well as to spiritual insight and "graces." In the *Epistle* we are told that in order to arrive at this final stage of "noughting" we must put aside "all the subtle and quaint imaginations or meditations that man can tell or find written in a book, be they never so holy, nor show they never so fair to the subtle eye of (man's) curious wit" (*Epistle*, ch. 9).

But here he goes on to say that such things were and are necessary in the early part of the journey, and we have here a principle which underlies all the "destructions" of the Cloud and of all Christian mystical writing. It may be called "the ladder principle" and indeed the image of the ladder was commonly used by these writers. Just as each rung of a ladder, even the lowest, is essential to the climber but must yet be left behind, so too the spiritual climber must use material and spiritual creatures and conditions in order to advance, and yet must, at the right time, leave each of them behind as he advances to the next step, which must in turn be transcended.[2]

---

[2] It must be said however, that there is a danger in using this image, or any secular image, unconditionally. For the steps are not so much left behind as subsumed, so that they are

This principle is important in understanding what is meant, in the quotation at the head of this section, by the destruction of "the naked knowing and feeling of thine own being." It is precisely this naked knowing and feeling that is the supporting rung or platform (extending the ladder image slightly) of the whole "work" of the *Cloud* and the *Epistle*, the work of cleaving to God by striking at the cloud of unknowing with a naked intent of the will. This is assumed in the *Cloud* and carefully spelt out in the *Epistle*. There it is explained that in fact the "naked intent" which pierces the cloud is "nought else to thy thought and thy feeling but a naked thought and a blind feeling of thine own being." (*Epistle* ch. 1). This thought and feeling is "naked" in that it is "not clad in any quality, as with the worthiness of thy being, or with any other privy condition that belongeth to the being of man." (*Epistle* ch. 6). So man in his naked being seeks God in *His* naked being, and this seeking is in and through man's naked being; it is the very *intent* of that being. Moreover this intent which is man's naked being becomes in this "work" entirely "oned" with the naked being of God. The author is careful to point out that this "oneing" is by grace and not by nature. (*Cloud*, ch. 67). Yet by grace it is a real "oneing," and the *Cloud* is here well within the

not really steps, and the ladder image breaks down. We have to think also of a growing organism, such as a tree and how each new "moment" of growth includes all that has gone before. In this subsumption and transposition of the very "humblest" elements lies a large part of the "glory" and meaning of the human world. Nothing is lost in the great transformation of time into eternity. This is perhaps the main affirmation of T.S. Eliot's *Four Quartets*, and it is significant that at the turning point of the fourth Quartet he quotes *The Cloud* ("with the drawing of this love and the voice of this calling" ch. 2). Yet it must be admitted, I think, that the author of *the Cloud* is so intensely upward-looking that he tends to forget the lesser glories of what is hidden in the "cloud of forgetting." I return to this point in the final section.

tradition of divinisation which will be reaffirmed in the 16th century by St. John of the Cross.

There is an ambiguity here. On the one hand it looks as if the naked intent takes us all the way into the full oneing and the "high alling." (*Epistle* ch. 6). Yet since the naked intent involves precisely the thought and feeling of one's naked being it is that which must be "destroyed." The author is quite firm about this: "this knowing and feeling must always be destroyed, ere the time be that thou mayest feel verily the perfection of this work." (*Cloud*, ch. 43).

I am not sure how far this ambiguity may be finally resolved. I shall return to it later. For the present I want to examine more carefully what the "destruction" of "this knowing and feeling" involves.

We are told (*Cloud* ch. 44) that the destruction is bound up with a special sorrow which is a special gift of God. It is a sorrow that is "strong" and "deep" and "ghostly," quite different from other kinds of sorrow, being at once more terrible than any other sorrow no matter how great, and more deep and intricate, a sorrow in the very depths of the spirit. "All other sorrows in comparison with this be but as it were game to earnest" (*Cloud*, ch. 44). This sorrow is grief for sin and sinfulness, but it is much more than this. It is a sorrow that is "full of holy desire" (*Cloud*, ch. 44), that is to say of desire for God, desire to escape from the knowing and feeling of the self and enter fully into the knowing and feeling of God. For "this is the true condition of a perfect lover, only and utterly to spoil himself of himself for that thing that he loveth, and not admit nor suffer to be clothed but only in that thing that he loveth; and that not only for a time, but willing to be

enwrapped therein in full and final forgetting of himself."
(*Epistle,* ch. 8).

Yet the thought and feeling of oneself is cruelly hard to
shed. It not only weighs on the aspiring spirit like a heavy load,
but it cleaves intimately to the spirit, being in fact the spirits
deepest holding of itself in its own selfhood, in its own
identity. The author of the *Cloud* sees the "holding" selfhood
as a "foul, stinking lump," and he gives a lively description of
the struggles of the lover of God to rid himself of the lump: "he
goeth nigh mad for sorrow . . . . he weepeth and waileth,
striveth, curseth and denouceth himself" (*Cloud,* ch. 44).
Perhaps one can understand this harsh way of seeing the
matter if we think of the subtle shifts and stratagems of
self-love among the "unco guid," and of how possessiveness
flows in even to the inner sanctuary of complete self-sacrifice
(as St. Paul notes I Cor. 13.3). All the same, I think it can also
help to see the "weeping and wailing" more sympathetically,
to see these tears of final self-relinquishment as full of pathos
and poignancy, full of the glow of sunrise. Yet it is a most
bitter thing, *the* most bitter thing, to leave oneself, where there
is no question of an "as if," of any kind of game, but rather is
the self faced with the stark, unbearable reality of its own
annihilation, entirely and forever.

At this point it is necessary to distinguish two kinds of
self-relinquishment, that which moves away from self-
consciousness and that which moves into it. I can drift off into
unconsciousness quite happily, as I do when I fall asleep, and
in a sense it is all the same whether I ever again wake up or
recover self-consciousness. So, too, I can sink my self-identity
in the group, ideologically or even orgiastically. Sometimes

this kind of "letting go" may be therapeutic; sometimes it is destructive. It has nothing to do with the self-relinquishment of the mystic. This latter is entered into in the fullest consciousness of the self in all its preciousness and pathos; in its memories; in the hunger for full (eternal) existence; in the deep caverns of its suffering, and the deeper springs of its substantial joy. In the mystic all the human energies are in full harmony, in full focus, in full clarity, in full power. It is at the highest point of this individual poise and power that he has to relinquish himself totally and forever. Indeed it is precisely his sense of the glory of Being in his own being that forces him onwards to affirm Being beyond his own being. He must die in order to live, but this is not bodily death but total death, the relinquishment of his being for the sake of that Being which calls him out of his being.

In taking this final intolerable step he is affirming not only God but the world and all that is in it, all creatures, all his fellow men in their individuality and special uniqueness and pathos. So far is the mystic from selfishness and "private" spirituality that it is he alone who is fully and entirely at the service of his neighbour. Contrariwise, the man who forgets himself in some ideology carries along with him that great lump of selfishness of which our author speaks, and this selfishness will sometimes grow to monstrous proportions as it takes to itself the energy of the group, and will always tend to do this, and will do this to whatever measure it can: a Hitler or a Stalin will become a great monster; the others will become little (or lesser) monsters. The mystic on the other hand will spend for others that energy already given to them in the giving of himself to God. He is Maximilian Kolbe or Edith Stein, waiting for death among the doomed, and supporting them; he is Bonhoeffer in prison radiating wisdom and power. Such people have at least entered into the way of final liberation.

Our author is careful to say that this relinquishment of the thought and feeling of one's own being is by no means an unmaking of one's being, an absorption of man into God. He uses the same phrase in the *Cloud* (ch. 44) and the *Epistle* (ch. 8) to make this clear. In the *Cloud* he writes: "And yet in all this sorrow he desireth not to un-be for that were devil's madness and despite unto God. But he liketh right well to be; he giveth full heartily thanks unto God for the worthiness and the gift of his being, although he desire unceasingly for to lack the knowing and feeling of his being." In the *Epistle* to "un-be" is likewise seen as "madness and despite unto God." To "un-be" is, if one may use the term, an ontological state, while self-relinquishment is a state of mind. It is possible to relinquish all thought and feeling of one's being without in fact ceasing to be. There is at first sight a contradiction here, for how can I relinquish the thought of my being while refusing to entertain the thought of my "un-being"? Surely what flows in when I relinquish the thought of my being is precisely the thought of my "un-being." I think that our author would admit this, but would say that nevertheless I do not, in fact cease to be, rather am I finding my true being precisely in thus relinquishing my being. For of course I affirm my being in the very act of relinquishing it, for this is *my* act, *my* giving up of myself. It is in this act with all its pathos and poignancy that I am most truly myself. It is in his prayer in Gethsemane and in his final words of dereliction and "letting go" on the Cross that Jesus is most touchingly and admirably himself; and this is true in their various ways of all the great Christian saints.

Weaker spirits may break at this point, or before it, and become as it were fragmented or "insane," yet even here there is surely some partial achievement, some prefiguring of that self-relinquishment in which the self is liberated from the weight of its self-involvement, and released into the clear air of the divine mystery, released (to use our author's imagery) into the light beyond the cloud. In thus losing his "life" man gains his "life," as Jesus said.[3] Yet the man who has come to this point of self-realisation is already very strong, and so the word "weaker" is purely comparative. What must be said is that we are here at a point of maximum pressure, of intolerable strain, and that one has to think of the possibility of breaking. One has to face the agonising question as to whether finite spirit can sustain this final transforming encounter with infinite goodness and holiness and love. Almost all the great Christian mystics agree that this is doubly impossible to man.

---

[3]Matt. 10.39 etc. Although the Neoplatonic influence is strong in the *Cloud* and *Epistle*, it is nevertheless true that it is possible to base all that is said on the Christian Scriptures, and in fact the author is conscious of this all through. It would be interesting to investigate the use of Scripture in the Christian writers of the Dionysian tradition. It would become clear, I think, that there is a twofold use of Scripture: a literal and a mystagogic. In the literal use texts such as that quoted above (another is Matt. 16:24 quoted in *Epistle* ch. 8) are used in their ordinary literal sense (which can of course involve metaphor) yet with a deepening of this sense in the mystical direction. This use may be exegetically controversial but it is usually defensible, and indeed becomes very persuasive if we accept a mystical atmosphere as surrounding the person of Jesus of Nazareth. The mystagogic use of Scripture infuses a mystical sense and direction into texts which in their literal context seem to be saying something quite different. Thus Jonas in the belly of the whale is seen as undergoing the experience of mystical darkness, as also Job and Jeremias. The *Song of Songs* is no longer a love poem in the ordinary sense but a celebration of the mystical marriage. Some mystical writers—John of the Cross, for instance—will claim that these interpretations open up the truth or hidden meaning of these passages, but it must be admitted that biblical scholarship is not nowadays willing to go along this road. Perhaps it would be the better for doing so, at least some of the time.

"The Drawing of this Love and the Voice of this Calling."

The author of the *Cloud of Unknowing* stands within the main Christian tradition in the matter of grace, on the whole leaning rather to the side of Augustine (i.e. the later Augustine) than to that of Pelagius. Grace understood as God's action and initiative is present at every stage of the journey: of himself and by himself man can do nothing. "But truly without him it is nought that we do, himself saying: *Sine me nihil potestis facere* (John 15.5). That is to thine understanding: without me first stirring and principally moving, and ye only but consenting and suffering, ye may do nothing that is perfectly pleasing to me" (*Epistle,* ch. 10). But in this matter we must distinguish between the active life and the contemplative life, both lives being understood in religious and Christian terms, symbolised by Martha and Mary. In the active life man himself is the principal agent, and God is present by sufferance or with consent, by sufferance in the case of sin, with consent in our good deeds. It is worth noting in passing that our author is anxious to guard the people of God against *merely* holy prelates: in all active services skill, wisdom, energy, must be given first place, for the "active" (as such) cannot depend on the divine initiative: he himself is the principal agent and he must be up and doing, looking to God's blessing and consent in all he does well, and subject to God's reproof in what is ill done.

In the case of the contemplative, on the other hand, it is God who is the principal agent, taking the initiative in all this "work," leading man onward by the drawing of his love and the voice of his calling (*Cloud*, ch. 2). "In deeds that be contemplative he is with us principally stirring and working, and we only but suffering and consenting: to our own great perfection and ghostly oneing to him in perfect charity" (*Epistle* ch. 10). Later the Spanish mystics were to draw a distinction between active and passive contemplation, a distinction which in recent times sparked off a sharp controversy as to the status of the mystical life in Christian spirituality. Active contemplation was in the ordinary way of Christian life and prayer; passive or mystical contemplation came with an infusion of the divine presence, which involves a special kind of feeling, of peace, joy, strength, etc. The symbols of light and fire were commonly used to describe this experience, as was also the bridal imagery of the Song of Songs. The question at issue in the controversy of fifty years ago was whether the mystical way was normal or abnormal, whether most people could go all the way through active contemplation with faith, hope, and charity, and the Christian virtues, or whether this way in the nature of things led on to passive or mystical contemplation.[4]

It might be argued, I think, that the author of the *Cloud* sees both of the two higher states (of the four named in Chapter 1: Common, Special, Singular and Perfect) as coming within what he calls the contemplative, which he sees as passive: "we only suffering and consenting." "Seest thou not how sweetly and how graciously he hath privily pulled thee to the third degree and manner of living, the which is called *singular*? In the which solitary form and manner of living thou mayest

[4]For a reasonably objective account of this controversy see Gabriel of St. Mary Magdalen O.C.D. *Acquired Contemplation*, Mercier Press (Cork) 1947; also R. Garrigou-Lagrange, *The Three Ages of the Spiritual Life*, Herder (St. Louis) 1948.

learn to lift up the foot of thy love, and to step towards the state of degree of living that is *perfect*" (*Cloud,* ch. 1). It would seem that from singular to perfect the divine initiative increases and the human contribution becomes more and more one of receptivity and obedience: the image that emerges is that of a child taking its first steps.

So, to return to our main theme, it can be said that the final liberation, from the thought and feeling of one's own being, requires not only ordinary divine help (as in everything to do with salvation) but is deeply set in the atmosphere of God's power and presence and man's weakness and fallibility. One could perhaps develop the image of the child taking its first steps by saying that here at the point of self-relinquishment man steps out into the void depending only on the everlasting arms. Yet this image won't do quite. For in trusting God man still hopes to have himself, to be restored somehow in his own individuality, and this implies an attachment to the thought and feeling of one's own being. The final liberation goes beyond this.

Here we must recall, I think, the dramatic descriptions in both the *Cloud* and the *Epistle* of the distress of the perfect disciple who "goeth nigh mad for sorrow" (*Cloud*, ch. 44). "Yea, Jesus help thee then, for then thou has need. For all the woe that may be without that, is not a point to that" (*Epistle*, ch. 8). It must be noted that all this distress comes from what is *being done* to the disciple by God, that he is not doing anything but only consenting to it. No self can relinquish itself according to this full relinquishment of the full self, the self achieved and grounded in substantial joy and peace. Only through the dark, "clouded," utterly mysterious vision of Love in its drawing and calling can the self be led through this narrow gate. For this self-relinquishment is not a game in the sense of a lover's game. It is not an *as if*. The disciple does not simply put himself in the position of relinquishing all thought and feeling of himself knowing all the time deep down that God will restore him, that all will be well for him. He does not relinquish the thought of himself as if it were merely the *thought* that was in question. No, he relinquishes all of himself, letting not just the thought go but letting himself go. There is no way in which he can *do* this; the most he can manage, and that with the greatest distress is to allow it to be done to him. "Father if it be possible let this chalice pass from me, yet nevertheless not my will but thine be done" (Luke 22.42). The Christian mystic who has come to this point of the challenge of "unselving" always finds in the prayer of Jesus in Gethsemane his refuge in the place of no refuge.

St. John of the Cross uses his favourite image of the Dark Night to describe the divine action and presence in this final phase of the spirit's ascent to unity. This is the passive Dark Night of the Spirit, at once annihilating and transforming, the deepest suffering leading on to substantial joy and peace. This darkness is so terrible that in its deepest intensity it lasts only a short time or else the soul would die. "At times it is so keen that the soul seems to be seeing hell and perdition opened."[5] And John uses the striking image of "a man suspended or held aloft so that he could not breathe." Also the Jonas image of a man buried alive in the depths of the earth or the sea, fully and intolerably alive in the utter loneliness of a world empty of God and all goodness. Thérèse of Lisieux plunged in this crucible in her last months kept on saying: "O my good God,"

[5]*Dark Night of the Soul* 2.6.6.

as if striving to affirm the goodness of God against the darkness, somehow creating that ultimate goodness and love anew within her own darkness.[6]

"This high alling of God"

In the third chapter of the *Cloud* our author sums up the advantages or fruits of this work of contemplation according to the mode of unknowing. It is a conventional passage, lacking the freshness and verbal panache that distinguishes most of his writings,[7] but it is all the more interesting for that, as witnessing to the traditional Christian attitude to the interior life, as other-regarding and as providing the greatest possible service to the community. "This is the work of the soul that most pleaseth God. All saints and angels have joy of this work and hasten them to help it with all their might. All fiends be mad when thou dost thus, and try for to defeat it in all that they can. All men living on earth be wonderfully helped by this

[6]See N.D. O'Donoghue *Heaven in Ordinarie* (Clark, Edinburgh; Templegate, Springfield 1980) pp. 70 ff.

[7]The language of the *Cloud* and the *Epistle* is direct and simple with a stream of fresh and striking phrases rising constantly into poetry by way of skilful alliteration, an alliteration at once free-flowing and unforced, unexpected and inevitable. This latter quality is especially true in the *Epistle,* and a quick reading of any chapter of that treatise will reveal it. It is worth noting that when the author, in chapter 10 of the *Epistle,* engages in a quite essential but rather heavy theological disquisition he apologises for this, being clearly conscious that he has fallen short of his own high standard of writing. Lightness, strength, economy, grace, freedom: these are some of the qualities of his way of writing. I feel that among the great mystical writers only the Lady Julian and Teresa of Avila match our author in this matter. Yet there is a difference inasmuch as one senses in our author immense erudition and sophistication in the background, held in reserve as it were, present as a kind of Flemish landscape, whereas in the case of both Lady Julian and St. Teresa there is question rather of a natural eloquence and finesse.

work, thou knowest not how. Yea, the souls in purgatory are eased of their pains by virtue of this work. Thou thyself art cleansed and made virtuous by no work so much. And yet it is the lightest work of all, when a soul is helped with grace in sensible list; and soonest done." (*Cloud* ch. 3).

The reference to "all men living on earth" is especially significant. It has been a presupposition of Christian mystical theory and practice from the beginning that there is an inner world of causality, a secret flowing of service and support in which the main agent is contemplative prayer. The main agent, that is to say, from the human side, for of course the divine action was seen as paramount. It was assumed that a certain human element or coefficient was essential to the whole process of grace. It was as if the divine love and power sought for a point of entry or points of entry, sought for a human response through which to operate. In silence, suffering, and self-forgetfulness the contemplative provided this response, provided it ever more fully as he himself became "divinised." He becomes an intermediary between God and men, thus being linked to the prayer and the mission of Jesus. A twentieth century Carmelite mystic, Elizabeth of the Trinity, speaks of the contemplative as another Christ, another humanity in which God renews the mysteries of Christ, this of course in and with and through *the* Christ, Jesus of Nazareth. At the base of this doctrine is a very strong conception of the unity of man, "the communion of saints," the mystical body of Christ. This concept is in fact worked out in the passage quoted above, not just the unity of man but the unity of all creation. Yet the author admits that in the last analysis this whole world of spiritual interflow is mysterious—"thou knowest not how" it all comes about. He is, however, quite firm as to the reality of it all, quite firm that the contemplative is doing a great work for the whole world of souls.

Yet for our author and the whole Christian tradition, the love and service of the neighbour is firmly subordinated to the love and service of God. To arrive at that state in which God is all, at the level of the "noble noughting" of the self and all else the "high alling" of God, in which God is all and nothing else matters: this is the deepest meaning and purpose of contemplation, of the "work" described in the *Cloud* and *Epistle* (e.g. *Epistle* ch. 6). Here we have a happy blending of the Christian "first commandment" and the Neoplatonic flight upward to the One. For both traditions the "alling" is absolute, for all else is valued or seen to exist only in the light of the Supreme Being, or the One beyond being. In all this mystical tradition it is a delicate and difficult matter to judge the value of creation in its own (derivative) being. Sometimes creation seems to be despised and disregarded, seen as a snare and a delusion. Yet, on the whole it is the mystic who most fully responds to nature; through this union with God he comes to see nature and even the world of men with a new openness and appreciation. A modern mystical writer, Thomas Merton, in his first book, *Elected Silence,* rejects the world and all its works, and sees it as full of vanity and ugliness; then after ten years or so in a contemplative monastery, he suddenly begins to see the world as a glorious place and ordinary folk as quite beautiful: this is a main theme in his later book *The Sign of Jonas.* In relinquishing the "world" as possessive and possessed the mystic finds it in its truth as mirroring the divine.

So, too, with the self. He who loses his life shall find it. It is in relinquishing the self that a man becomes truly himself, becomes truly the image of God, sharing indeed in this high alling. For the alling is also a oneing, an indissoluble marriage of man and God, an entry into the joy, peace and glory of the divine being. This is not the "un-being" of man's being, but rather its fulfilment. What seemed the undoing of man was the highest doing of God in man.

In my end is my beginning.

T.S. Eliot's *Four Quartets* is a contemporary meditation on life in terms of the *Cloud* and the Dionysian tradition of Christian mysticism.[8] The final definitive quartet, *Little Gidding* hinges around the phrase from chapter 2 of the *Cloud* already quoted which speaks of "the drawing of this love and the voice of this calling." It is this phrase, used by Eliot as a sort of incantation, that resolves the final tension of the poem, that of holding and letting go, recalling and reliving the past or leaving it behind to fare forward into the future. In the drawing of this love and the voice of this calling there is the offer at once of liberation from the past and its restoration. To answer this call, to enter this love is to reach the "end," but it is also to recall, restore, and restate, the "beginning" and all that has intervened of feeling and striving. In a poem called *Ithaka,* the Greek poet C.P. Cavafy sees *Ithaca* not as a place at which one arrives, but as the journey to Ithaca fulfilled: Ithaca and the journey are one. So for Eliot the condition of "complete simplicity" which "costs not less than everything," and is achieved only through a "lifetime's death in love," includes all that has been done and suffered.

[8]Faber and Faber 1976 (9th impression).

The author of the *Cloud* is a man in a hurry; he travels light; at the end nothing is left but God; God is all in this "high alling and noble noughting." He does not explain that where God is, nothing is lost. And it must be admitted that at this point he is very much the Neoplatonist for whom everything fades into darkness in the light of the One. Yet I feel that if he were pressed he would agree with Eliot that there is a vital distinction between "detachment from self and from things and from persons" and "indifference to self and to things and to persons." The cloud of forgetting does indeed seem to imply indifference, but our author's concern is detachment, and what it makes possible. Self-relinquishment as he describes it is a dramatic and terrifying experience, pointing not to emptiness but to a larger fulfilment. He does not say that everything has finally its place in this fulfilment, but I feel he would not at all deny this if challenged.

There is one further point which Eliot also helps us to focus. The end is the beginning not only in that it includes the beginning (and all that follows), but in that man is always beginning. It is easy to get the impression that the author of the *Cloud* has arrived and that the disciple is *en route.* Again Neoplatonism (and the Dionysian tradition as commonly understood) gives this impression: thus John of the Cross can speak of the "top" of the Mount of Perfection. And perhaps our author wants us to see it thus. Yet I think it is clear that the "work" described, when it has been done and suffered, is but a preparation and initiation. For one thing the negative "unknowing" side of the work is but temporary. Even though our author is more anxious to have the disciple leave aside his "proud, curious imaginative wit," and all that comes under the name of "understanding" in order to leave room for this "work" of seeking God by the "naked intent" of the will, yet he admits that this is but a temporary state: "let thy wits fast awhile, I pray thee, from their natural delight in their knowledge" (*Epistle* ch. 13). It would be wrong to underline "awhile," yet it indicates what the author takes for granted, that the work of reflection and "understanding" continues and that the man who has begun to live in the "cloud" does not thereafter live in the clouds, that every end is a new beginning. Perfection is never perfectly achieved: there are always new heights to scale.

Yet to say this is perhaps to push the author further than he would wish to go. In fact we are here touching a large question in relation to which our author is an ambiguous witness. In the physical order man grows to full stature, and then he rests from growth; he is an adult, a complete human being. Does the same hold true in the spiritual order? The Christian mystical tradition speaks with two voices on the subject, and it would seem that the Dionysian strand in this tradition answers "yes" to the question. Yet the sign of the Cross lies over everything in Christianity, and the Cross always lies ahead, with always beyond it the Resurrection.

What then of liberation? There is a sense in which it can be achieved, in which it is always in a measure achieved as the pilgrim progresses. Yet there is a sense in which it is always in question, always dependent on divine grace, and this at all levels. The converse of this is that the final liberation, "this noble noughting and this high alling," is available in some measure to every man.

8

The Sword of Peace
Some Reflections on Christian Pacifism

In the Fifth chapter of the Gospel according to Matthew, Jesus calls down a blessing on those who bring peace (literally, "the makers of peace"); a little further on, in chapter ten, he tells us he has not come to bring peace down on the earth, but rather to bring a sword of division that reaches right into the heart of families, dividing father and son, mother and daughter, everywhere dividing one from the other, so that a man's enemies are to be found within his own household. Here we have an ambiguity or a paradox, perhaps a contradiction, that seems to run right through the Christian centuries, in which men have preached peace in the name of Jesus Christ, and equally made war in his name, in which his power and presence seems to have bound people together and, equally, divided them one against the other.

Let us in our effort to see clear invoke the Holy Spirit, and consider how this same Spirit is identified with peace. We find this identification expressed very vividly at the end of the Gospel according to John, in that powerful and moving passage where Jesus appears to his disciples huddled together in fear behind barred doors (20:19). Suddenly he is there, right there with them. Like the loved one who has died in that saddest and most peaceful of love-songs *She Moved through the Fair,* he too "came in so softly his feet made no din." But he is no mere appearance, or rather his appearance is more powerful than the total reality of the situation. For he brings peace with him, and this peace strangely radiates from the wounds in his body, the wounds from which the blood has flowed. It issues also from his mouth as sound and as breath: *Eirēnē hūmin,* "Peace unto you" is the sound they hear, and with it the breathing and the naming of that breathing as the Holy Breath, the Holy Spirit of God. The more we allow this passage to permeate our inner ear, the more we truly become hearers of this word, the more we see that the peace in question here is nothing like the mere absence of strife, nor yet is it any positive *quality* however excellent. Rather is it a substantial reality, a reality of immense power, making inexorable and even awesome demands on us who are not yet wounded, whose blood is all within us, perhaps frozen or clotted in ungivingness: in fact a divine reality at once all pervasive and as concrete and sharply pointed as a sword. A divine reality at once cosmic and personal: the Holy Spirit, that Person who creates personhood in each of us, as St. Paul tells us in the Eighth chapter of Romans. We do not really know ourselves in our deepest selfhood where we open to that Fathering Beauty whence we come: it is this sword-sharp, all-filling, all-encompassing Spirit that creates us as full persons and partners in this encounter (Romans 8, vv. 14 to 16 and 26 to 28).

So the Spirit for the Christian is Peace, and thus a most mysterious *Reality* that shatters all our human notions of what peace is and is not, what it demands and does not demand. So the Christian pacifist is a man possessed, a man taken over by a world-shattering force, world-shattering and world-creating. He carries a sword that divides and disturbs, that penetrates into that inner reality which is that fear in each of us that keeps the doors locked and barred. But in dividing and disturbing, it *reveals* a false peace and a false security, as of a boatful of people drifting happily towards the Niagara Falls. A mighty wind blows the boat another way: some accept this, some resist it with all their might. This in fact was the situation described in the Prophet Micah (ch. 7) which Jesus recalls in that passage in which he says he comes not to bring peace but the sword (Mt. 20, 34), a situation in which a whole people had turned aside from the Lord of Glory and Peace, a situation which could be healed only through disturbance and turmoil. Yet through this disturbance the people's sins are "cast into the depths of the sea" (v. 19). The Spirit moves over the deeps of chaos to create a new world.

The Christian pacifist will then have nothing to do with the subterfuges, adjustments, political expedients, by which people evade their own deepest reality as children of the Father of universal love, of total generosity. As they are makers of true peace, so they are breakers of false peace. For them the bomb and the bullet and the bayonet are blunt weapons which can neither pierce the heart of man nor do anything to save him from what is truly to be feared. In that same chapter ten of

Matthew's Gospel Jesus tells us clearly what is truly to be feared: the wrath of the living God which is no more nor less than the love of the living God. The Christian does not preach Gehenna, but he bears witness to the truth as he sees it; he calls things by their proper names, and so he is a disturbing presence among men and women. He carries around with him the Sword of Peace, which is a Sword of Light that intolerably reveals the dark places of the heart. Yet it also reveals the deep fountains of tears and blood flowing within us; for we have forgotten how to weep, as we have forgotten how to shed our blood, that we might affirm in our time and place the peace that flows with the Blood that flows from the Cross (Col. 1:20; Eph. 2:14).

Where then is the Christian in our great debate about nuclear war and disarmament? He is already gone to war, like the Minstrel Boy in the Irish ballad, and with something of that same reckless courage and wild joy. Wherever he is he stands for truth and justice and honesty and the call of the Living God to total sincerity. He may through a kind of innocence or misplaced loyalty join the wrong party, but he will press relentlessly towards sincerity, consistency, self-sacrifice. He will not easily accept a slogan like "rather be dead than Red," for he knows that the only death worth looking at is that spiritual death which is no more heavy over Poland just now than over England or America. He will be just as appalled at a nuclear holocaust in Russia or China as in France or Britain: if and insofar as he is the least bit less concerned about Russia than about Britain, the least bit less concerned about other people's families than his own: to this extent he is false to his Christian commitment, and to this extent his arm lacks power in wielding the Sword of Peace. For the Holy Spirit is no respecter of persons, but is the maker of true personhood all over this planet. He is the Breath of Christ that radiates with infinite gentleness and power from the wounds of Christ. The Christian pacifist is the man or woman who is open to the Holy Spirit and its absolute demands of honesty, truth, courage, and joy.

9

The Place of the Angels

A World Without Angels

For many years now I have been able to set aside a natural tendency to worry about having too much to do in all sorts of ways in relation to time and energy, and I have placed all the business of my life in the hands of the angels, those marvellous friends who are somehow present here as I write in West Pilton Circus, Edinburgh, Scotland. Like a schoolboy I feel like going on to add Great Britain, Europe, Planet Earth, The Solar System, The Milky Way, The Universe. For the mention of angels places one immediately in a cosmic situation, at once overwhelming and exciting. The ancient philosophers and astronomers attached one or more angels to each of the heavenly bodies. These were the angels of the spheres, and one of their functions was to make music, the Music of the Spheres. Their main function, however, was to guide and harmonise the various parts of the universe, having special care of this precious and unique earth on which man lives between birth and death.

Alas! For scientific man all these Shining Ones have died long ago. Not only is Pan dead, and all the nymphs and satyrs and dryads, but Gabriel has also passed away, leaving Mary of Nazareth bereft of her heavenly child. So has Raphael, leaving travellers with their air-tickets and Michelins. So, too, has Michael, guardian of the shores of Ireland, Brittany and Cornwall. So truly has Michael vanished that a Pope could visit Ireland for the first time in its dolorous and heroic history without mentioning Michael even once, without casting one glance towards that mighty wave-tormented rock named Michael's Skellig off the South-West Coast of the Island of Saints and Scholars. Pope John Paul came and went, and said many words and was photographed several million times, but he said not one word of Michael, nor did he come within fifty miles of that ancient shrine of Michael where Christian monks lived and died for centuries, far out in the sea. Yet as it happened the day he came was the great ancient feast of Michael, September the 29th. He came at Michaelmas and no one noticed the day nor saw any significance in it. For even in those Celtic lands where once Michael (and all the angels) was known and loved men no longer have eyes for these heavenly guides and companions.

Of course it must be said that these Celtic lands, Ireland, Scotland, Wales, Cornwall, Brittany, are now for many centuries the graveyard of the most dynamic civilisation this world has ever known, the civilisation which lifted Europe out of the Dark Ages and brought to birth Modern Europe with all its greatness and misery. This Celtic world now lies buried deep and seems entirely dead. With it the angels have vanished from Christendom. Yet the voices of this world are not all stilled; a few gentle scholars have brought them to us, have bent down and listened to the lost words of a dying culture and have written these words for us to hear. The greatest of these scholars was Alexander Carmichael, a man who deserves to stand with Rudolf Steiner, at the doorway of this century, as a herald of the angels to a people who have forgotten their best friends.

The Celtic Angels

Alexander Carmichael (1832 to 1912) was a Scottish civil servant who devoted all his spare time and retirement to collecting Gaelic poems and stories in the Western Islands and Highlands of Scotland. His six-volume collection (with translations) entitled *Carmina Gadelica* has saved a vast amount of oral tradition that was on the way to being lost forever. These poems and stories (poems mostly) provide a vivid portrait of a great Christian culture passing into oblivion. With the three twentieth century classics, *The Islandman, An Old Woman Remembers* and *Twenty Years Agrowing,* that came out of one small island on the South West Coast of Ireland (now inhabited only by cattle) they provide a noble and enduring epitaph of a culture which reaches back to the dawn of European literature.

The first two volumes of *Carmina Gadelica* were published in 1899, and reprinted in 1928; two more volumes were published in 1941, and a fifth in 1954. There is also a sixth volume of appendices. Carmichael provided a literal English translation of the material; more recently G.R.D. McLean has published a poetical translation, using Carmichael's Gaelic text.[1] A selection from *Carmina* was published in 1960 by the Christian Community Press under the title *The Sun Dances,* and this is still easily and cheaply available. A glance through any of these books will show that the angels are everywhere in these old Gaelic poems and prayers, coming and going as naturally as they ascended and descended upon the Son of Man (John 1, 51). They are invoked in all kinds of blessings in the company of the Three, and of Mary, and the Son of Mary, of Joseph and the Apostles. It is a world of good companions. As he came to be oppressed and exploited the Gael lived in thatched cabins and rude hovels, but his habitation was full of shining presences, and he carried the light of heaven in his heart. That chameleon writer, Flann O'Brien, has written a brilliant satire called *The Poor Mouth* in which he "sends up" the literature of the bad old days of the Gaelic world. Both the satirist and the writers he satirises miss what may be called "the quality of the light", the way in which a situation of massive oppression and economic misery was overlighted by the heavenly presences. Viewed in relation to this overlighting the Marxist and Freudian analyses of religion seem particularly inept: there was no pie in the sky, for the sky was under the roof; there was no father-figure to give security and comfort but rather a whole company of holy beings visible only to the inner eye of love and self-giving. There was, of course, plenty of what is called magic, some of it rather dark, and plenty of what is called superstition, but these were diseases of a basically healthy organism that the modern world has killed.

[1]G.R.D. McLean, *Poems of the Western Highlanders.* London: S.P.C.K., 1961. In the case of the poem quoted above I made my own translation of the Gaelic text. It is perhaps worth remarking that the introductions to all these books are worth reading—that in *The Sun*

Of the many poems and prayers I might choose from the
Carmichael harvest to illustrate the presence of angels in this
ancient world now passed away, I choose one called "Michael
the Victorious." This was written down from a crofter's wife
in South Uist and will be found on page 105 of *The Sun Dances*.
It is a poem of clear, strong images, at times splendid and regal,
at times close to the common sights and sounds of nature.

> Stand guard all around
> O Michael Victorious
> On your bright shining steed
> With your sword that tamed
> The dragon. Your name:
> Great Ranger of heaven
> God's Warrior Man.
> Be thou at my back
> O Michael Victorious;
> O Light of my Days
> Thou shining and glorious
> Guard me always.
>
> My round I will make
> With my saint by my side
> On machair, on meadow-land,
> On the cold hills of heather;

Dances is by Adam Bittleston of the Christian Community. Carmichael's own introduction is not only informative but, in places, extremely moving. McLean remarks that the
poems of the Carmichael collection are superior in strength and freshness to similar
collections from Ireland such as Douglas Hyde's *Religious Songs Of Connacht*. I think the
reason for this is that Irish Catholicism absorbed and institutionalised the Celtic tradition,
whereas in the Scottish Highlands and Islands pockets of the common people resisted the
Reformation, and so remained in touch with their far past.

We'll travel together
Round this hard globe of earth.
No harm will come to me,
For your shield is over me,
O Michael Victorious
Light of my heart
O Michael Victorious
Shepherd of God.

I think we should pause for a moment to salute Janet MacIsaac, the crofter's wife who lived her very simple life in the aura of this noble vision. I think even the sceptic will admit that there is a kind of direct evidence of final truth in noble words and images, and in the clear eyes that express them. And the Christian must ask himself whether a poem like this is superstition or pleasant fancy, or rather a restatement of a theme that is not far from the centre of the experience of the first Christians. Indeed we know from the early accounts we have of the Christ-event that Jesus, for all his divinity, was helped in his time of deepest agony by an angel, and that he had a special word to say about the angels of little children who "always see the face of God" (Matt. 18, 10.)

What is most of all clear from this poem and the other poems and prayers of the Carmichael collection is that the angelic world was, for these people, as much part of their lives as the hills and the seas, and the daily pains and ardours of human living. They bring to our depaganised and dechristianised imagination the challenge of a way of life suffused with heavenly colours. In this rich fabric nature and grace are most wonderfully, and indeed most curiously, blended. Long before the time of Patrick, long before the great event in the East, the hills and seas were full of heavenly presences. Nora Chadwick, the Celtic scholar, speaks of the beauty and dignity of these presences.[2] It is as if Michael and all the angels were already there, revealing their true identities only when Christ the true sun (as Patrick calls him) shines across the land. So it is that as we listen to these poems and prayers we feel that the hills and the rivers and the windy uplands are full of voices, voices fresh and clear as the air of the Land of Youth, and yet as old as origins. These voices come faint and muffled in translation; in the Gaelic as in Hebrew the words seem to come straight from the Elohim, the makers of heaven and earth at the beginning.

Angels and the Theologian

Of course this consciousness of angelic presences and the invocation of their aid was by no means confined to Celtic Christianity. It is a substantial part of the Christian heritage East and West, and has in thinkers like Aquinas a formidable theological backing. And, of course, this tradition is still alive today. A few days ago I visited a family of Chilean refugees. The father is a Marxist, but his 10-year-old daughter was proud to repeat in Spanish an invocation to her guardian angel, which she says night and morning. Catholic children are still taught these invocations, though much less than formerly, and with less conviction on the part of parents and teachers. Preachers have little to say on the subject, and theologians tend to dismiss it in a paragraph or two. The

[2] *The Celts,* Penguin 1970. "A beautiful dignity hangs over Irish mythology and orderliness, a sense of fitness...The heathen Irish erected a spirituality—spiritual loveliness which comes close to an ideal spiritual existence."

Scripture scholars have cast out angels from the New Testament as if they were devils. Catholic dogmatic theologians tend to admit the reality of angels, but seem to regard them as somewhat embarrassing supernumeraries. They are there in their own sphere, but man must make his own way on the earth: his task is to build the earth, admitting other worlds and even some kind of heaven when his earthly task is done. To focus on other regions is to miss the whole meaning of life; to look to the angels to do my work for me is to opt out, to live in a world of dreams. Thus Karl Rahner is ready to defend quite strongly the reality of angels, but cannot allow them any real place in the Christian, or any other, way of life.[3] They are a kind of decorative adjunct to Christian doctrine, not really relevant to a Church come of age.

Now I want to take along with me Rahner's defence of the reality of angels with its massive background in Christian, Jewish and Muslim tradition, and to challenge his attitude to their relevance and helpfulness to contemporary man. Indeed I want to attack this kind of assertion head-on, and to affirm not just its contradictory but its contrary. I want to say two things: first, that in the individual life an openness to the spirits all around can transform our attitudes and activities in direction of wholeness, creativity and an *agapé* at once costing and joyous; second, that the future of planet earth is no longer in the hands of men and women who try to build a better world together—for we have already passed the point of no return towards catastrophe—but depends entirely on whether men

---

[3]See "Sacramentum Mundi," under "Angel." For a more positive approach see Heinrick Schlier's book *Principalities and Powers in the New Testament* (Bunn & Oates, London 1961), in the Quaestiones Disputatae series. But Schlier is primarily concerned with the hindering and destroying angels.

and women call in the angelic powers to save this planet, to lead it on to a more spiritual age.

Before I try to elaborate this double thesis I want to look at one quite strong objection to my whole enterprise which will be put forward from certain Christian standpoints. Briefly: Protestants will say, "Surely Christ is sufficient for all our needs"; Catholics will say "Surely Christ and his Blessed Mother are sufficient for all our needs." In reply to this I would say that the really continual Christian affirmation is that the Word of God, at once *with* God and God in his own right, became man as Jesus of Nazareth, who by his life and death transformed this earth. But this transformation, from sin to justice, from darkness to light, did not and does not *coerce* man in any way. It leaves him free, and works out his freedom within the world of this darkness: only now he knows that the light is there for him to appropriate. He must bring light into his own life and into the world around him. In this world man is in the body, and so he must attune himself to the conditions of the body. If I want to go to London from Edinburgh, I do not ask Christ to transport me there, even though I believe that Christ has come in the flesh, and does in fact live in the body, and is everything to me at all levels. This is just part of what the incarnation means, and the Word in Himself and *in me* is subject to the limitations of the flesh. Now man is spirit as well as flesh, and is, in the nature of things, just as much subject, in his spirit, to the conditions of the spirit-world as he is, in his body, subject to the conditions of the material world. It would be just as absurd for him to bypass the world of spirits as to bypass the world of British Rail and the Health Service. Yes, God can work miracles, but the greatest, most tremendous miracle of all is creation itself, including the world of the

Celestial Hierarchies with their marvellous scope and power in the universe, and their direct relationship to man and to this most precious earth. They are part of this mighty harmony of innumerable regions and orders of being, as we too are part of it.

So it was that the Word made Flesh, Jesus of Nazareth, who asked a woman for water when he was thirsty, could also be helped all through his life by the spirits that surrounded him, could be helped by the good spirits as we are, challenged by the evil spirits, as we are. Indeed, we do but understand the half of the Christ story if we see it only in terms of the historical-visible. Rather did the Logos become man at two levels, that of the spirit and that of the body; and at least as much happened at the one level as at the other. The Gospels are indeed written from the standpoint of the historical-visible but they are not by any means enclosed by this, as we in our technical age tend to be. So it is that we miss the "openings" into the invisible that come again and again in the New Testament. These openings accompany Jesus all the way from his conception by the ministry of Gabriel to his ascension when he, so to speak, passed through the threshold of these openings and the "two men in white" spoke to the disciples of the Second Coming.[4]

Those who refuse to open to this world of openings do but read the half of the New Testament, and so reading it miss much more than half of its atmosphere and scope. That is one

[4]Is it possible to make any sense of this return of Christ apart from the angelic spirits that will surround it? (Matt. 16, 27.) It is presented not as a destruction of earth but as the final and complete opening of heaven into earth, an earth which, as Teilhard has seen, reaches to its own limits. At these limits is the opening, the world of the angels, a world invisibly present all through the New Testament.

reason why our theology today rarely causes the reader's heart to burn within him as he reads.

A Very Present Help

And now at last to my double affirmation concerning the present helpfulness of angels.

First, I say that the contact with the angels can transform the life of the individual Christian. All I have been saying from the standpoint of theology, and, earlier, from the standpoint of Christian traditions, should give a substantial background to this claim, enough perhaps for me to say: "Try it for yourself." This means giving angels a place in your inner life of prayer and meditation, in that activity wherein the mind seeks its own centre, where it reaches inwards to the Source. When Jesus used the words "in the heavens" in his invocation of his Father and ours, he is not using a merely decorative phrase. In the context of the New Testament (and the Old) the heavens had a definite meaning, referred to a special region with its own atmosphere and its own citizenry. Jesus did not address a lonely figure in an empty sky, the First Mover of Aristotle or the One of Plotinus (though, indeed, it is we rather than the Greeks who have isolated the God of the philosophers). He addressed the Lord of Spirits, the *I am* whose angels stayed the hand of Abraham, and appeared in the Burning Bush (Acts 7, 30), the Lord who rides above the Cherubim, the Lord God of Hosts. All this and more is expressed in that first invocation of "our Father who art in the heavens," and leads us to open ourselves to the ever-present household of the Father of our

Lord Jesus Christ.[5] It must be remembered that we are free, and that our freedom is sacred in the eyes of the Father and his angels. So we are given only what we freely ask for in the full sincerity of filial asking. But if we ask, we shall receive.

Here it is worth recalling that when Jesus is being done to death he does not say: "The Father can save me" but rather does he say: "I can ask the Father and he would send his angels to save me." (Matt. 26, 53.) It is the Father we "ask," and all prayer goes on to the Father, yet even here the angels are our helpers in presenting our asking and our adoration. So it is that the angels have an important place in the ancient Christian liturgies, East and West. In the traditional Eucharistic prayer the priest asks that the angel of the Lord may carry the sacrifice to God's altar on high; some of us regret that this invocation has dropped out of the New Catholic Mass Rites in the Second, Third and Fourth Eucharistic Prayer.

All prayer goes to the Father, but this does not at all mean that we cannot contact the good spirits that surround our lives. These beings are as real and as available as our doctors, lawyers, bank managers; indeed they are much more available, for we can contact them merely by opening our minds to them. They cannot, nor do they wish to, change the great lines of our destiny, however seemingly dark this may be at times, but in all else they are constantly and delicately helpful. They are in my experience particularly helpful in matters that concern human attitudes and emotions and human relationships; again and again they clear the air; again and again in

[5]The Greek of both versions (Matthew and Luke) of the Lord's Prayer has "en tois ouranois" which is "in 'the heavens'," not "in heaven." The Latin and the French get it right.

speaking with people in distress I have been marvellously helped by them to ask the key question, or open up some line of thought or emotion.

If I were asked to describe the nature of this angelic presence in human relationships and encounters, I would use two words to describe it: *peace* and *transparency.* By peace I do not mean a neutral quality or atmosphere, the mere absence of strife or tension. Rather it is one of the richest and most varied of human dimensions. W.B. Yeats speaks of a peace that comes *"dropping slow/dropping from the veils of the morning to where the cricket sings,"* and this peace of a quiet island in a dark clear lake in the early morning is indeed special and sacred. The peace in question here is quite some distance on the spectrum from that island peace: its best image is the freshness that enters a smoke-filled stifling room when a window is opened, or suddenly swings open. It is the peace in which communication is possible because a closed self opens a little to another person, and so to the whole universe. And the activity by which this happens is imperceptible; the window swings open noiselessly. There is no sense of the extraordinary, of a miracle happening. At least I have found it so; and I find it so. I can only say to you: "See for yourself; open to the world of the angels, not as a game or by way of curiosity, but in all sincerity, and you, too, will find it so." One thing, however, must be said: this is not an easy way to spiritual power. The only true way to spiritual power is the way of the Cross, the way down into weakness which is the way up into power. The angels were with Christ all the time, all the way, but they did not carry his Cross for him, or save him from weariness, distress, disappointment, and something that was near to despair. Yet he was the light, and the angels were an essential element in that light. Through them we reach towards that same light that has its centre in him.

So much for the presence and place of angels in the life of individual persons, and in personal encounters and relationships. It is an important presence and an important place, but what I want to speak about finally is far more important: it is the presence and place of angels in the cosmos, and especially in Planet Earth. One does not have to be a Nostradamus, or an Edgar Cayce, to see that Planet Earth is facing catastrophe. For the first time in history (as far as we can discern) man can destroy this sure and firm-set earth, can turn all its freshness and teeming fulness of life into a slag-heap. We are left with Isaiah and the son which he named Shear-Yasub which means "a remnant shall be left." No more hope for the future than this one child of catastophe. Perhaps for all we know, Shear-Yasub is already conceived, and we are facing that immense holocaust which will leave but a weak remnant of a civilisation whose final deed of power was to destroy itself.

In this situation it is clear that everything depends not on the mindless computers but on the minds of the men who control the computer. If we are to avoid this catastrophe we need a change of mind which is also a change of heart. We need a spiritual awakening, a spiritual opening. Now my main contention all along, a contention based on the Christian scriptures and more than amply verified by personal experience, is that man in his spirit lives and moves in a world of spirits. But man is also free, the individual man and the totality of men. The angels will not intervene, *cannot* intervene, unless man makes with them vital enabling connections. No angel will reach down to switch off the computer, though such an intervention is possible on the wings of prayer, as when Peter was released from prison. What the angels can do most naturally is to clarify the spirit of man, to open men's minds to the light of God which shines around them. That white light of the Godhead is too much for man; it reaches him through these spirits that are only a little above him. They are the clouds in which Christ is coming; they herald his Kingdom across the centuries and millennia. If he were to come today or tomorrow the planet would shrivel up before him, and only the few could look on his face. At times the New Testament seems to say just this, but He who comes is infinitely patient and compassionate, and he sends his angels before his face to prepare the way for his coming. But man is free, always free; and in his freedom he can reject or fail to make contact with the angels of God.

One way or another the Christ will come. He will come not in judgment, but in love, but it may happen that he will *seem* to come in judgment, so that men wither away in fear and expectation. The Day of the Lord is also the Day of the Angels, as it is the Day of the Woman Clothed with the Sun. Herein is found the only protection for sinful and imperfect men and women. Herein we see the only harmonious way forward for this planet. The alternative is a world purified by catastrophe.

Those passages in the Scriptures which talk of "sendings" and messengers are very profound. One can ask: why does not the Lord come Himself as He is? The reason is that the Infinite beauty, purity and pathos of God is far, far more than man can take. Were it to bear down suddenly on man's ugliness, selfishness, and hardness, what would be left of the great majority of men? So we must reach up to the Holy Ones among us here on earth, and to the Invisible Holy Ones of the

Angelic Hierarchies. So it is that we must have messengers, that God's relationship with man is by way of "sendings."[6]

That is what an angel is, a messenger of the divine sending, God's fingertips, a touch at once immeasurably firm and infinitely gentle. In a certain general and yet quite real sense all creation is a sending. As I sit here at my window I hear birds singing and trilling and I look at a tree in full greenery. These are messengers from the same divine source as that from which I too have been sent, as Christ has been sent and the Holy Spirit. Between these two orders of sending, the visible and the divine, is the great world of discarnate spirits, the living dead who once walked the earth—these are sometimes called Ministering Angels, by Shakespeare for instance—and the spirits of the Celestial Hierarchies. They are not a kind of ornamental addition to the Cosmos, but are intimately part of it. Without them man's life is full of emptiness. Without them Christ is forever uncomforted in Gethsemane.

---

[6]At the source of all "sending" is the Breath of God, the Holy Spirit of God. All the Angels may be seen as breathings of this Eternal Spirit. But the relationship of Pneumatology to Angelology is a separate unwritten chapter of Theology. The cosmic struggle outlined in the Book of Revelation and elsewhere in the New Testament gives an added urgency to what is said below about the planetary aspect of the invocation of the angels.

10

Sister Death

Attitudes to Death

All philosophy, said Plato, is a meditation on death. In our own day Heidegger has reiterated and restated Plato's affirmation, with the difference that death now seems to triumph over the philosopher, his philosophy being no longer a reflection *on* death but rather a reflection *of* death.

In between stands Francis of Assisi, for whom death is neither an enemy to be overcome nor a fate to be accepted but rather a friend, a kinsman, to be received with all courtesy. Not just a kinsman either but a kins*woman,* towards whom courtesy takes on the added grace of chivalry. And not just a kinswoman but one bound in to my life by the closest bonds of nature and nurture—Sister Death.

It is with Sister Death I am concerned in this meditation, with death as born into the same household as man. In reality the members of a single family live together for a while under the same roof, and then usually go their separate ways. But sometimes they maintain a close contact, and it is this kind of relationship Francis seems to imply. Sister Death is always at hand, a life-long companion.

Before going on to reflect on this companionate view of death, I want to salute in passing the other main attitudes to death which we find among the living.

I have mentioned already the philosophical attitude and two main varieties of it, that of Plato in which death is transcended and that of Heidegger in which death provides a transcendence which it destroys. It is doubtful whether Heidegger's attitude is finally coherent, and one can ask how far some kind of concept of survival is implicit in the whole thrust of his philosophy. But this, as Aristotle would say, belongs to another line of inquiry.

Distinguishable, though not always distinct, from the philosophical attitude, there is the tragic view of death, the pathos and poignancy of death expressed above all by the poet. "One night awaits us all," says Horace, "and one eternal sleep," and a thousand poets great and small have added their voices to this lament for the passing of life and love and all the dear familiar world, all that belongs to "the warm precincts of the cheerful day." Pathos flows into the void left by the vanishing significance of all that was so dearly and hopefully planned and wrought. The lights go out one by one to the very last, the lights of friendship and love; and as each light vanishes it becomes an arrow that pierces the heart in that most terrible piercing that is sheer and clear poignancy. My little life becomes a rivulet that joins the great river of tears that is human history. The poet finds some relief in the creative expressing of this tragedy. Yet all he tells us is that the tragedy is pure tragedy, without the least relief, for him or for us.

The tragic attitude to death accepts death as it accepts tragedy, as part of the human condition. Indeed it is sometimes seen as the only issue and resolution of the evils of life: "the close of all my miseries and the balm" for Milton's Samson. Here the poet "all passion spent" sits down with, or stands beside, the Stoic philosopher.

But there is another attitude which disowns or disdains this kind of cold comfort and simply refuses to accept death or come to terms with it, rather with the woman in *The Waves* of Virginia Woolf, "flings" itself against death, or with Dylan Thomas "rages against the dying of the light." One simply rejects death, fights it, hates it, struggles against it to the last, refuses to accept it either for oneself or for others. Death is the enemy, obscene, abhorrent, an unjust and shameless aggressor, usurping the place of life. To domesticate death by seeing it as part of life is to play the coward, to bow the knee to a tyrant. It is an attitude at once childish and noble, recalling in its latter aspect the Celtic fairy-tale about the youth who attacked the Mountain of Fear and Destruction that had destroyed all his companions. The youth's desperate daring won the day, but nobody can gain the victory over death.

And yet some Christians will say that this is precisely what Christ has done, gained the victory over death. Indeed a certain strand in the Christian theology of death agrees entirely with the rejecting attitude set forth above, sees death (i.e., physical death) as the result of the Fall, and its destruction as the final act in the redemptive work of Christ. Much Eastern Orthodox theology and a strong tradition within Protestant theology looks at death and redemption in this way, and indeed there is much in St. Paul to support this viewpoint. It is bound up with an outright rejection of Greek humanism with its doctrine (in Plato and his school especially) of the natural immortality of the soul. This is condemned as dualism, and as involving the kind of naturalism that makes nonsense of redemption in Christ. Indeed, this kind of theology is at its best in drawing a sharp distinction between Christianity and Hellenism, and between theology and philosophy (to the disadvantage of the latter). It is at its weakest in making sense of the fact that Christians die like everybody else and that death seems to have been life's companion long before man appeared on this planet. Besides it is not easy to dispose of all those men and women, good and bad, who had no contract with redemption through Christ.[1]

The thesis that man is by nature, or at least by his fallen nature, mortal, and only immortal through Christ, is not *necessarily* linked with a rejecting view of death, yet there is a real affinity between the two. Death in this view, is of itself utterly destructive, and does not, by any means, find a place within the transforming experiences of the spirit's life. All is darkness and pessimism except through the great miracle and mystery of the redemption and resurrection by which death has itself been put to death: *mors mortua est.* So, all natural values, all merely human goodness and greatness are null and void. One sees how this thesis links up with the central Reformation assertion of the uselessness of "works" and with the still honoured phrase, "the filthy rags of human righteousness." It is easy to take the further step and say that natural

[1] For a strong contemporary statement of this viewpoint see Oscar Cullmann, *Immortality of the Soul or Resurrection of the Dead?* (London: Epworth Press, 1958). See also John Hick's *Death and Eternal Life* for what might be called a more balanced view, though Hick in trying to avoid dualism is forced to speak of a dramatic "reconstitution" of the personality after death. On the other hand the Westminister Confession seems to accept the natural immortality of the soul (ch. 32).

man can contribute nothing to his own salvation, not even the free acceptance of this salvation. And, of course, the next logical step is either to say that some are saved and some condemned (to hell) by divine decree or else that all are saved in the long run, willy-nilly. We find Barth in his *Humanity of God* being forced to the latter alternative.

I do not wish to explore this matter any further here. What I wish to make clear is that the rejecting attitude to death can count on a good deal of support from theologians in the Reform (and Greek Orthodox) tradition; I wish to say also that in this matter I take my stand with the opposing (Hellenistic humanistic) thesis, though I hope that what I have to say about death may not be without interest for those who hold to the "supernaturalistic" position.

All these attitudes, the philosophical, the tragic and the rejecting, I feel I can identify with, and thus, at least partially understand. But there is another attitude, or sheaf of attitudes, which I cannot identify with, and which I can only try to state without real understanding. This (or these) might be labelled "indifference," the attitude of those who do not see death as really significant or important, for whom the question of survival is of no real interest. Such people are not usually indifferent to life, nor do they lack energy, nor a deep sense of moral value, but they are content to live within time, taking each day as it comes, accepting the death of friends as part of the process of day to day living. They may mourn death, but this does not really open up any final or metaphysical question, or if it does, they quickly return to ordinary living and the ways of everyday practical wisdom. Sometimes this attitude is bound up with a strong sense of the community or family or collective as the great fact within which the destiny of the individual is integrated and given its true and only significance. This would seem to be the attitude of Marxism and other totalitarian systems.

Linking this attitude to the philosophical (which indeed is very varied) is that moral puritanism or purism which insists that virtue must be its own ground and its own reward. Kant the moralist tended to this view even though Kant the metaphysician was forced to postulate immortality as the necessary ground of duty and moral activity. As a moralist he insists that the good must be done *because* it is the good and not because of its repercussions in the world of eternal life. The moralist who is only a moralist will in fact tend to rule out immortality *a priori* and see death as the proof positive that virtue is its own reward, in other words, see death as a kind of purifying angel. A contemporary exponent of this view is Iris Murdoch, a professional philosopher who is best known as a novelist. In her *Sovereignty of the Good* she argues for what she calls "the pointlessness of virtue," that is to say that virtue can have no end or purpose beyond itself, if it is to be true to itself as virtue.[2] This thesis is worked out in all sorts of situations in her novels, and it is usually accompanied by a good deal of more or less bitter reflection on death, but at the end a kind of indifference towards death emerges for the key character, who by deep suffering has come to see that love or humility or "the good" in one or some of its other aspects, is all that really matters.

These, then, are some of the attitudes which men and women come to adopt towards death. The list is not meant to be exhaustive, nor are the attitudes mutually exclusive.

[2] *The Sovereignty of the Good over Other Concepts* (Routledge & Kegan Paul, 1970).

Neither do I wish to distinguish too sharply my own attitude (or, rather, the attitude to which I subscribe) from all of these: it is in fact close to Plato as well as being (I will claim) radically Christian.

The Dark Companions

Everybody from time to time finds himself walking with a companion or companions that he would dearly like to shake off, destroy, somehow escape from. All are unwelcome; some are abhorrent; a few are utterly devastating. Some of these companions—grief for instance, or anguish—come and go. Others, such as fear, may be always there, at our side, sometimes vocal, more often quiet. Some, such as those already mentioned, may be more or less universal; others, such as panic, depression, or, despair, may be specially yours or mine.

Most people can cope with these companions most or even all the time. But there are some who cannot cope, cannot cope at times, or cannot cope at all. Every psychiatrist, every counsellor, every priest, is meeting such people almost every day. These people are not different from the rest of us in having to endure the presence of the dark companions, the only difference is that they cannot cope, or find themselves in a situation where they (or perhaps anybody else) cannot cope.

These companions include not only feelings but also realities, the great realities of the human condition: pain, failure, disease, poverty, oppression, exploitation, war, natural catastrophes. Above all, death.

Nascentes morimur: death is born with each of us, life's inseparable companion, always at hand, invisible at first, but gradually revealing itself as the glow of childhood fades into the light of common day. And once it has revealed itself it never goes away, not for one moment, until the moment when it takes us into its kingdom.

Yet, for all its uniqueness, death is but one of the dark companions of life, and it cannot be truly seen or truly understood by itself. We must, therefore, look at this wider companionship more closely.

And, first of all, we must draw a clear distinction between life's dark companions and life's evil companions. These are: hatred, jealousy, bitterness, possessiveness, and the rest. These are at hand for all of us, most persuasively or speciously at certain times and in certain connections; and for each of us there is at least one of them that seems to have allies within the heart, so that we can shake off this companion only through a great struggle that may leave us weak and spent but happily victorious. For all these companions are destructive of all that is precious in the Kingdom of the Spirit, and we must fight them to the death if we are to be free.

These evil companions bring with them their own special atmosphere of darkness, always menacing, sometimes strongly seductive. "Pray that I may not become bitter" said Teilhard de Chardin shortly before his death to a young friend: for all his scope and depth of mind he recognized the seductiveness of this darkness even in old age. Now this atmosphere, this darkness is entirely different from the darkness of the dark companions. The darkness of grief or anguish or fear is as different from the darkness of bitterness or jealousy or hypocrisy as day differs from night, as white from black. For the dark companions show themselves as angels of light, and we begin to glimpse the possibility that perhaps, after all, those that seemed enemies may be friends, may be, somehow the good companions of life's journey, or at least may belong with such good companions as joy, love, hope and liberty. The image of death as the Grim Reaper dissolves and is replaced, if not by Sister Death, at least by a figure that is somehow familiar and friendly.

By a figure above all that has a *right* to be there. If we take man as he is, as he has emerged from the biological stratum of this planet, it is clear that he is cradled in death, that the death of others serves and conditions his coming, that each individual man is, as it were, placed and planted by the death of those who have gone before him. Only thus can he inherit the earth in his own time, in the generation of his maturity. Only thus can he be father and mother in full maturity and independence, ruling his household, reliving, recreating, and refashioning culture and traditions. All those precious things by which a house becomes a household, and a man master thereof, are gifted by death, the death of past generations, and held in trust, and not as possessions, because I too must die. Death gives, and in giving teaches me to give, teaches me the generosity of the *gens*. Thus by all that is dear and familiar in life, death has a right to sit by my fireside.

So, too, the other dark companions have a place in my life if only because of the gifts they bring with them. Fear protects me; anguish chastens and purifies; grief deepens me; desperation shows me new paths, makes me surmount what seemed insurmountable; panic guides my hand towards the other, and the others, and the Other.

Stern companions they are certainly. They do not flatter me. "No man jokes with death" said Don Quixote at the end. Neither does a man joke with desperation, nor with grief. Yet, for all that, the other, good companions of life are never far away: joy and celebration and all that man as *L'Allegro* can call upon, even "laughter holding both his sides." As these merry companions dance and sing, death seems to have been banished and forgotten. Yet I recall a eulogy by an Irish writer, Bryan McMahon, on an Irish dancer of the *Siamsa* group who had died, in which it is averred that the Irish dancer with his still hands and expressionless countenance points towards the quiet of death while his feet tell exultantly of life. Death has not been banished. She is there and she is part of the dance as she looks on, affirming balance and ultimate harmony. When, as in the *danse macabre,* death is pulled in to the frenzy of the dance, man has lost his balance and his bearings. He has allowed the evil companion to lay hold of Sister Death. And what alienates man's everyday self from his deeper self is the dark masquerade in which some evil companion wears the mask of a dark companion, as when cowardice wears the mask of fear, possessiveness the mask of grief, envy the mask of anguish, bitterness the mask of death. Death in itself *as* death is, however terrible in seeming, a force that binds man into his deepest self, a rending of his everyday being that is an unveiling of his deepest being.

Weakness and Strength

Death is the final, total, unalterable, inescapable, weakness of humankind, and a meditation on death must be, centrally, a meditation on weakness.

Human weakness, like all other human dimensions, is at its deepest and purest, mystical, that is to say bound up with that state in which man meets God as flowing and communication. Every true mystic understands this, none better than St. Paul (unless it be Jesus himself) in the Christian tradition. It is a Pauline theme usually overlooked or obscured by commentators who, in any case, miss the mystical (and therefore the very core) of their author. Two of his statements are especially significant, the paradoxical "when I am weak, then I am strong" and the mysterious "power is made perfect in infirmity."[3] Paul's strength is, of course, the strength of Christ, by which Christ lives in him and he in Christ. But this strength is *the kind of strength* that is made perfect in infirmity, the kind of strength that belongs to a man choking to death, alone and forsaken by man and God, utterly helpless: Christ crucified. This is the highest strength that Paul knows. This is the strength that reveals itself to him in his own weakness, that achieves its perfection in perfect weakness. Here for Paul is God, at once infinitely strong and infinitely weak, infinitely

---

[3]"Horror and dismay came over him, and he said to them, "My heart is ready to break with grief" (Mark 14:34). The two nouns of this (NEB) translation seem to me to translate accurately the verbs used in the Greek. "At midday darkness fell over the whole land, which lasted till three in the afternoon; and at three Jesus cried aloud, *Eli, Eli lamma Sabachthani*, which means "My God, my God, why hast thou forsaken me?"' (Mark 15:35, NEB). It seems to me that the various efforts to soften this text tend towards a trivialization of Christianity.

strong only because he is infinitely weak, infinitely weak only because he is infinitely strong: no man could be strong enough to undergo this weakness. No, nor to overcome it by strength, as if the weakness were absorbed by the strength. No, not that, not that at all, but rather strong enough to *be* so weak, to *have* being in that very abyss of weakness, to enter therein and inhabit that weakness. Who is there who could not, would not share omnipotence, exult in the creating of a million worlds? Let God but call to the sharing of his strength and we all get up at once and run "as giants." But who amongst us can or will answer the call to follow him in his weakness, into his weakness?

Yet that is the call, to follow him, to be like him, to be sharers in the divine nature. How terrible, how intolerable! How far beyond my strength is this weakness! Only by his strength can I share his weakness. Yet what if his strength is but a fuller, deeper immersion in that same weakness from which I have turned away in terror? There is indeed an almost intolerable temptation here to look for an easy way, for cheap grace, for a sharing in the divine nature which is not really an entry into the fire of that unbearable goodness and love. But there is no easy way, nor will there ever be here or hereafter, for God does not hand out self-contradictions. He can only give us himself by giving us *himself*, at once infinitely weak and infinitely strong. It is in whatever fleeting glimpse he may have of this most mysterious coincidence of opposites that man comes nearest to apprehending the essence of God.

Only love can bind together these opposites, a love strong enough to undergo all weakness.

But no limited, human love can stretch as far as this. For a while, to the measure of his love, a man's weakness goes hand in hand with his strength. But at some point, soon or late, finite love fails and he is unable to travel further into the depths of weakness, nor can he continue this journey unless his love grows deeper. Yet, always, Infinite Love calls him onward, and new horizons of freedom unfold. This call is the call of Love, call to fuller communication, fuller receptivity. Here all is gift, but the gift is a sharing in the giving, in the supreme giving of oneself. Grace, the divine gift is not like the gift of a house or an earthly kingdom. It is the utterly terrifying gift of God himself, utterly loving, utterly self-giving. This love binds our strength and weakness together, manifests itself in the ways of weakness, of death and annihilation, is yet of itself eternal and immeasurable.

This love and this weakness are utterly open, utterly exposed, utterly vulnerable. The spirit that flies from this weakness turns into itself, seeking strength where it is not, affirms itself as total being, as possessing and dominating all around. This is the way of what is called moral weakness, and it is the very antithesis of that true weakness which is the secret of the mystic, the secret revealed by Christ in his passion and death.

The Death of God

Christianity rests on the affirmation that God has died, or more exactly, since God is outside of time, in the affirmation of the death of God. In this lies its uniqueness, its power, its pathos, its depth, its utter mysteriousness, and its truth. Indeed to speak of uniqueness or "particularity" at any other level is to reduce religion to the status of an examination paper, or a kind of salvation supermarket. God calls all men to himself (and each man to his "ownmost" self) in a marvellous and entirely admirable variety of ways, but who can travel all the way into that uttermost pain and loneliness and dereliction, into the 'horror and dismay' of the unmaking in Gethsemane, into the final annihilation of the *Lamma Sabachthani*?[4] Who can travel the way of Love to the end? It is here that Jesus is the only way, the guide who is still with us and ahead of us, the one man who can carry the full burden of this love.

Recently I saw a television programme on the treatment of *spina bifida* children in which a doctor said that there were times when a doctor had to "play God." He meant that the doctor could decide to "put the baby to sleep" if it would not anyhow survive and this, as he saw it, was "playing God." I am not concerned here with the moral issue, at least not directly, but with the terrible misunderstanding of God involved in the phrase the doctor used. For if the Christian affirmation means anything it means that the role of God was being played in the very situation itself by the baby and its parents; at least they were being, so to speak, faced in the direction of God's presence, God's calling, God's loving, and God's strength. Along the route of the dark experience awaiting the parents (and the child perhaps) was waiting the divine love and the divine strength.

Traditional Irish Catholicism of the kind now on the way to disintegration, was severely restricted by chauvinism and triumphalism, but it did at least understand one thing: the infinite vulnerability and pathos of the "heart" of God. Devotional practices such as visiting the Blessed Sacrament

[4] 2 Corinthians 12.

(the lonely "prisoner of the tabernacle"), making acts of "reparation" to the Sacred Heart of Jesus, "doing" the First Fridays were and are, of course, open to abuse and parody, but they had and have at their centre a true feeling for the vulnerability of God. And as these practices recede with the passing of the last generation formed in them, we must ask ourselves whether we are in danger of losing touch with the God who became man and went forth to his death that the world might know something of the love that unites the Father and the Son.[5]

Christ announced his own death as the manifestation of a love that radiates to all, and indeed states as a principle that in the order of manifestation love at its highest and death are inseparably linked. "Greater love hath no man than this that a man lay down his life for his friends."[6] But the death which Christ will undergo is not either a simple falling asleep, nor yet a passing over to a better world, nor a returning whence he came (though he does, of course, say that he is "going to the Father"). No, it is a death that is also an annihilation, a death that, as it were, gathers into itself every possible weakness and dereliction, all that human ingenuity could devise to break body and spirit, to unman manhood and undo all aspiration to divinity. Worse still, much worse, it is a death presided over by "the powers of darkness" whereby the deep caverns of the spirit are invaded and occupied by a force destructive of all that is humanly precious and dear and familiar. The New Testament tells it four times, the terrifying story of Christ's death, tells it so powerfully that it is almost impossible for the Christian to escape its implications.

[5]John 14:31.
[6]John 15:13.

The Gospel according to John is a profound meditation on the death of the Logos, who is God and yet became man. Primarily this death is seen as a celebration of love. There is no question of scaling down or overlooking the weakness, abjection and helplessness of this death to make room for the glory. Rather does the glory reveal itself in the very completeness of the death and the dying. The devotional tradition of the Exaltation of the Cross has reaffirmed and developed this inexhaustible paradox over the Christian centuries. There are, of course, many other devotional traditions which explore and particularize this paradox, for example, the devotion to the Face of Christ Suffering dear to St. Thérèse of Lisieux, the Enthronement of the Heart of Christ, represented as pierced and sometimes as ringed with thorns. There is also a devotional tradition which has as its object the glory of the risen Christ, and in this tradition, as represented by Christian writers and artists, the wounds of the Passion are seen as centres of special radiance. In this tradition, especially as developed in the Easter liturgies, Christ is seen as the victor over death, as if this victory were his great and special achievement: *mors mortua est,* death itself died.

But this glory of triumph and victory must not be confused with the glory of suffering love. The two glories are distinct and complementary, and though one or other may be emphasised according to the liturgical cycle, or the needs and insights of men and epochs, yet there must always be a sense, at least tacit, of their balance and harmony. The glory of suffering love by itself does not reveal the variety and wild grandeur of creation; the glory of the Resurrection does not of itself shine into the deepest recesses of the heart, where the springs of both joy and sorrow have their sources. The two types of glory are as inseparable as life and death. Indeed it can be said that the one is the glory of life, all its colour and charm and exuberance, while the other is the glory of death, all its pathos and poignancy and gentleness. They are, as the writer of the Fourth Gospel saw, two faces of the great mystery and epiphany of love.

What he (and the others) was announcing was the new and perfect, the definitive and eternal *shekinah* adumbrated by the old, imperfect, temporary *shekinah* of the dwelling of Jahweh in the Holy of Holies. This was to be a true presence of the true God *within* the human, partaking of all the weakness and vulnerability of the human condition, and this not as an unfortunate, unavoidable implication of man's fallenness but as the very truth of real incarnation, as the verity of *verus homo*, and even more profoundly as the manifestation of God as Love, a manifestation which could only be by way of a revelation of an eternal twoness of lover and beloved, in complete reciprocity, an eternal act mysteriously yet necessarily completing a trinity of love.

The manifestation of eternal love in the weakness and vulnerability of the human condition (with all this entails of pathos and poignancy) is something freely admitted and affirmed by Christian theology, but there is very often a subtle docetism behind this affirmation. For the docetist, the incarnation is a divine game in which God *appears* to be man, pretends to be man, but is not really human at all, for he did not suffer or feel or think or will as a man. This is docetism in its obvious or crude form; clearly it dehumanizes Christ and empties the Incarnation of all real significance. But any kind of "decentring" of the humanity of Christ comes to the same thing, for the central divinity centres all else, and in doing so absorbs it.

So, Christ would carry his humanity as a man carries a child, sustaining all its weakness but not really sharing it. But if God is to be truly incarnate, truly a sharer in human weakness then, in some sense, the incarnation must manifest some aspect already there of the infinite hiddenness of God. We cannot pierce the veils that front this hiddenness, nor can we ever say what that which has been manifest is *in itself*. But as manifest it is weakness and vulnerability, the cry of a baby, the sigh of a weary traveller, the heavy perspiration of extreme agony of spirit, the loneliness, pain and dereliction, of death at its most annihilating. In this and through this, glory shines, the glory of suffering, self-giving, utterly sacrificial, love. As this dark glory reaches its own limit as total darkness it merges into that other glory which is new life, refreshment, joy, transformation, Resurrection.

The Death of Man

The Christian affirmation about man's destiny is that he passes through death to eternal life, which is the life of God. Man meets God, the living God, in God's life, which is new life for man. And to meet God thus in life man must pass through death.

But if the primary Christian affirmation is that God has manifested his being and his glory precisely in undergoing human death, then man encounters God as truly in dying as in "rising again" to eternal life. It seems, in fact, that when we compare death as we know it, mostly a very quiet "passing away," with the death of Christ, the man who is God, it must be admitted that most men enter only a little into the weakness, vulnerability, agony, loneliness and dereliction of the death of God, as perhaps, equally, most men do but enter a little way into the fullness of the life of God. This is indeed a terrifying thought for the "follower" of Christ, for the man or woman who would follow him all the way, who would "drink the cup" with him. We know that some have accepted this invitation in all its challenge and terror and have encountered extreme darkness and agony at the end.[7] But are all men somehow invited into these terrifying depths?

A certain kind of brisk Christianity will brush this question aside, and I have nothing to say to this attitude, except that I do not think one can deal briskly with death. I think the challenge and invitation of Calvary imposes itself not only on the follower of Christ but upon all who reflect at all deeply on life and love and death. For this reflection must take account of the kind of death-bed which can have significance only through the sign of the Cross. I may indeed "cease upon the midnight with no pain," but how can I propose this, and pray for this for myself and my friends, without proposing it also for all people everywhere and at all times? Without, in other words, proposing to undo the earth, without above all, reducing death to dimensions wherein there is no space for God to die? Does not any genuine reflection on death bring us to a point of decision, to accept death in its fullness and with its companions (even including terror and loneliness and dereliction) or else to reject it. And one description of the Christian is that he is the man who accepts death fully.

---

[7]See "The Greatness of the Little Way" in *The Furrow*, vol. 28 (1977), pp. 599-611.

Sister and Bride

The death of man is, as ending or termination, essentially the same as the death of an animal or a plant. The vital spark departs and a dead thing is left, a pathetic memento of what was and will never be again in this individual way. I have just returned from a journey to the Scottish Highlands in the course of which, near Birnam (of all places!) I came on a small wood that has been hacked down (to make, perhaps, a better road). The dismembered trunks and the lopped and torn branches seemed to cry out at their untimely and unnatural death. I felt I was living their death for these trees, assimilating it, absorbing it into my own death. Death might have come gently to these trees, as time's companion, in time's footfall, and I might not have encountered it as pathos and poignancy. Or it might have come through men who truly loved the trees they had to cut down, who would then have themselves known the priesthood of death. Then the scene would have been quite different, and I would not have felt the need to take this death into my own, undoing a desecration.

Man alone in this mortal world meets death face to face. Sister Death stands beside the tree as it grows, is there riding in her dark chariot as the bull charges into the ring. The woodman meets the death of the tree; the matador meets the death of the bull; when they are *true*, you can see death reflected in their faces; grave, peaceful, sacramental, mysterious. One of the strangest and most moving books I have ever read is the autobiography of Pierrepoint, the official executioner to the British and Irish Governments, and the last of a line of executioners belonging to the same family. It is clear that this man (and the tradition to which he—quite proudly—belonged) gave his complete attention, at once compassionate and exact, to his work not so much of death as *with* death, that somehow each meeting with another's death was a meeting with his own death. He did not in fact believe in capital punishment, but he did believe in the sacredness of death as he believed in the sacredness of life.[8]

Man, then, like all mortal things is born to die, but unlike all else (as far as we know) he is born to *meet* death, to live with death, the only choice he has is that of rejection or acceptance. He can treat death as an enemy, rather as *the* enemy, for this enemy relativizes all other (lesser) enmities. Or he can treat death as a familiar companion, Sister Death, who becomes at the end his sole companion, the consort in whose embrace he loses himself: *soror et sponsa.*

But, as T.S. Eliot saw clearly, for it is the burden of his *Four Quartets*, the end is also the beginning. Not in the sense, however true or certain this may be, that the end of this life is the beginning of a life "beyond death," but that death is there already as part of what life is and signifies, that mortal consciousness is a living consciousness of death. In this sense life encloses death, assimilates death, absorbs death. So when death comes it is but the fulfilment of life insofar as life has accepted death. As Heidegger saw, to be truly human is to accept one's human status as being-unto-death. But Heidegger did not see that the spirit that fully accepts death has by that acceptance overcome death, that it is in fact impossible that this spirit should itself die. The meeting of life and death is an event in *spirit*, in living consciousness.[9]

---

[8]*Executioner: Pierrepoint* by Albert Pierrepoint, Coronet Books, 1977 (1974). Writing of his attitude Pierrepoint says: "I always believed my craft was sacred."

[9]Wittgenstein's celebrated statement that "death is not an event in life" is either trivial

But death as seen and known is more than the shedding of the body, more than an event in the life of the spirit. Man is so fully incarnate that death faces him as complete annihilation. The philosopher or the religious man may indeed see death as a little thing, but the union of life and death is far more complete than that. It cannot be dissipated by thought however clear and trenchant, not unless a man relinquishes a great part of himself. The human spirit is incarnate spirit, and as such is intimately involved in the death of the body. I must face this extinction of my very self; I must *live* my death if I am to be true to my manhood. This is true, even though few men face it truly. We fly from death (I mean, of course, the *fact* of death as an inescapable future event) and so we fly from life. To live fully, truly, authentically, as Heidegger saw, is to look death in the face, and to allow it full scope as the extinction of my innermost being.

This is the Dark Night of the mystics in which the spirit loses hold of itself in extreme anguish. In this ultimate union of life and death the ego dies and a new being emerges, a being open to the universe, a "divine" humanity. The mystics do not say this occurs *at* death—I am thinking especially of St. John of the Cross, but if you look closely you will find it in all the great mystics—but through the full acceptance of death, through radical meditation on death. It may culminate in death, but this is, as it were, an "arrangement" by which the great Craftsman does his work in the "soul". The work is that of releasing the spirit, not from the body, but from the bonds of egoism. In this great work life and death are inseparable companions.

or false, trivial if it means that the event of death terminates life and so is not in it, false if it means that death is irrelevant for man in living his life.

I was, not so long ago, present at a death in which the young woman of twenty-five or so who was dying said: "I can die now because I can live." She had been a minister, and had assisted at several death-beds, but she could not accept death until she met her own death face to face. Then and only then she found she could live with death. So also she could die, for she had experienced deep within her the fruitful union of life and death.

For the fulness of life and the fulness of death go hand in hand. Only those who have opened to the immense harmonies and pathos of life, to the divinity of God, can open up to the negative dimension of the immensity of loss in the total extinction of our being. In other words, it is only the mystic who can fully experience the awful darkness of death, as it is only the mystic who can truly experience the Dark Night of the Spirit.

This is the *experience* of death at its deepest. It *may* coincide with the *event* of death, or it may not. Perhaps for some (for most?) it may come after the event of death, in what is called Purgatory. It is "the narrow gate" and a few there are that find it, as far as we can judge. Yet it is for all, here or hereafter.

Through this narrow gate the self-regarding, self-affirming, self-secure ego cannot go. This is not to say that the ego is somehow evil. By no means. It is the condition of growth, the place within which the spirit grows, the protective sheath within which this unique, individual human experience is created in freedom and grace. It is because of the light within that the lamp has to be shattered; it is because the poem of life must find its setting in the great harmony that it must become a word released into the void. It is because man is destined for divine fellowship that he must "leave the warm precincts of the cheerful day," leave it as a bride leaves the home of her childhood. The very pathos and poignancy of the leaving is part of this leaving: the heart must break if it is to open to the heavenly dimension.

It must be said, then, that the philosophical attitude to death (as represented typically by Socrates looking forward calmly and even joyfully to his spirit's release from the body) is not so much false as incomplete. It fails to see that physical death is but the external expression of a far deeper, more interior "letting go" and unmaking. So too is any Christian notion in which death has lost its sting, the sting of final self-renunciation, of an agony and anguish that has no comfort beyond acceptance in love. It is true that death often comes easily for the philosopher and also for the Christian. But when this is the case, the truth of death has not been encountered in this experience. And, in fact, this is frequently *not* the case: good philosophers and good Christians sometimes have terrible deaths. We need only think of the death of Jesus of Nazareth himself.

The Final Liberation

The Platonic philosopher sees death as liberation from the body; I have been trying to see death as liberation from the self, a liberation that, from within the self that has to die, can only be seen as infinitely pathetic and poignant. This infinity of pathos and poignancy has been the main theme of every great poet from Homer to Yeats or Eliot or Dylan Thomas. It runs, a great river of tears, through Virgil's *Aeneid* where one great line names it forever: *sunt lacrimae rerum et mentem mortalia tangunt* ("Here be men like ourselves, for they *know* death and the tears of things").[10]

Now one can ask *why* it is that sorrowful and destructive death should thus issue in that universal and immeasurable world of pathos and poignancy, and why especially this world should call forth all that is highest in man the maker and artist. Why this unending dialogue with beauty, present from the beginning and ever renewing itself in the succession of cultures and forms? Is not every true poet a priest of the mysteries of human destiny, and must we not listen to his words as to an oracle that has a deeper meaning? As we listen to the song of Polly Garter in *Under Milk Wood* lamenting her lovers and the one man whose absence fills her whole heart, as we listen to the voice of this very human pathos (*even* here I mean) do we not hear also, if we listen more deeply, the voice of eternal and deathless beauty, and is not this precisely what the poet has achieved, this surplus of *presence*? The death of the self is somehow intensely beautiful.

The self dies into its own fullness, its own divinity: that is the consummation. But the *way*, the transforming energy, the creative force in this great happening is *love*. It is not physical death, the shedding of the body, that shows "the greatest love," but rather the relinquishment of the self, that entry through "the narrow gate" where nothing remains except the deep inarticulate acceptance that is *radical love*. I die, but the world goes on. I accept this, and so leave my own self behind. Not only that: this love as it affirms itself, as it finds itself in its

[10]Aeneid, I, 460.

truth and fullness accepts death freely that the other (the "friend") may live. It is only here at this depth of entire selflessness that we can truly encounter Christ's definition of perfect love: "that a man lay down his life for his friends."

If, however, this death of the self is to be valid, as fulfilment and transformation, the self that meets it must be complete, must have attained, at all levels and in all dimensions, full humanness. The seed must die, but it must be truly and fully seed, for this seed is spiritual, and *so* free, and *so* self-forming. So it is that only the fullness of life (and this includes the joy of living) can meet death in its fullness. "Now I am ready to die, because I am ready to live."

The seed must die, but the seed is not destroyed. If you throw the seed into the fire, or hammer it into powder, it will bear no fruit at all. The seed that dies takes with it through its death all its characteristics down to the least item of "cellular memory." In fact its character, its inner being has been freed, given proper space and ambience.

So, too, the human self is not destroyed in its dying. All that marvellous beauty of pathos and poignancy is at once sunset and sunrise. This, of course, the Christian knows from the Christian promises, but I am saying that a true understanding of death reveals this in any case. Here as elsewhere revelation clarifies our natural vision, takes the philosopher further, but in the direction of his own keenest vision. Death is indeed a release, a liberation, as Plato saw, but it is a release not just from the body but from all that "holds" and limits us. Moreover, what is left behind is not cast away or "buried," but is rather liberated and discovered. All that we have been and loved and known goes with us into that purifying darkness, and emerges in the full clarity of universal love. This love is

now the very atmosphere of our being: it illuminates, penetrates, permeates everything. In accepting the whole I accept
myself, and so enter into my freedom.

This inner mystical death is, I say, the truth and fullness of
death of which physical death is a mere shadow or symbol,
though they *may* in fact coincide. Since mystical death is a
kind of annihilation (the seed "dying") we tend to see physical
death in the same way, and for some people no assurance can
really serve to change this attitude. They are being forced
towards a love which is its own ground. Their special anguish
is to see death as the end, as the utter annihilation and
relinquishment of the self, even though they may for the most
part succeed in keeping this anguish at bay. Their special
challenge is to affirm love and all positive values in the face of
this. Yet here it must be repeated that only those who live
fully can enter fully into death, can experience to the full its
pathos and poignancy. This is the way of the mystic who may
be in fact defined as the man who lives fully and dies fully:
next to him comes the poet, and indeed the two ways often
unite in the one person.

In death life reaches its own limits, and breaks through
these limits to freedom.

Death as an Enemy

If then death is life's companion and the way to life's
fulfilment, and if moreover death must be seen primarily and
properly as mystical and therefore transforming, why is it that
the New Testament sees death as an enemy, indeed as the last

and greatest of the enemies defeated by Christ? But if we look more carefully at the main statement of this doctrine, by St. Paul in 1 Corinthians 15, we shall see that death is seen primarily as the way of transformation. Indeed St. Paul uses the image already used by Christ himself, that of the seed which must "die" to become fruitful. Moreover, he draws a clear distinction between two kinds of death: ordinary death, and transition or metamorphosis. "We shall not all die, but we shall all be changed."[11] Ordinary death is part of a fallen sinful creation that awaits deliverance;[12] it is therefore counted among the enemies from which fallen man is redeemed by Christ: indeed it is the head and chief of these enemies, carrying the sting of sin and the power of Satan within it.[13] Christ defeats death, but he does not obliterate it nor change the fabric of the fallen world; rather does he, by embracing death, purify it and rediscover its inner transforming power as transition, as "the narrow gate" that opens on to the fullness of life.

We are here encountering rather acutely a tension that runs through the New Testament attitude to death. On the one hand death and the other dark companions of man's journey are enemies from whom Christ frees him (at least in principle); on the other hand it is by way of this companionship that man is led on to his fulfilment and transformation: it is good and necessary that the seed must die, the narrow gate is the gate of heaven, the straight and narrow path leads to eternal life. They are, it would seem, aspects of the great central mystery of love, the love that shines forth so gloriously

[11] 1 Corinthians 15:52.
[12] Romans 8:20.
[13] 1 Corinthians 15:55.

in the life of Jesus of Nazareth, most gloriously of all in his death and resurrection. The glory of his death and the glory of his resurrection seem at first sight as opposite as black and white, yet if Love is the supreme value, the supreme beauty, these two glories are the one Glory. And if Jesus is the Anointed One, God dwelling in our midst, then this is the way he has to go, into the "horror and dismay" of the Garden, into the dereliction of the *Lamma Sabachthani*. So it is written, "that the world may know that I love the Father."[14]

Waiting for Easter

This mediation on death has brought forward three main insights, which are imitations or "broken lights" rather than theological affirmations.

There is, in the first place, the distinction just recalled between the two glories, a distinction that seems to run through the whole of the Fourth gospel and is always *there* implicitly in both Old and New Testaments. There is the glory that shines out from the way of humility, poverty, suffering and death, the glory of the Suffering Servant of Isaiah, of the "lowly" and "meek" of the *Magnificat* and the Beatitudes, above all of the Passion and Death of Jesus, the Anointed One. There is, more obviously, the glory of Thabor and the Resurrection, of the great miracles, of the brilliant and powerful preaching of the Prophet from Galilee, who overtops all the great ones of the past, the glory of a personality that could draw men and women away from their work and

[14]John 14:31.

households, that is indeed still doing so today . . . These two glories somehow belong together, as death and life belong together. They are aspects of the one mystery.

Secondly, physical death, death-as-an-end, is but the outward expression and symbol of death as spiritual transformation. I have called this spiritual transformation "mystical death," for the power and terror, the reality and "glory," of this death is the main burden of some of the great mystical masters such as St. John of the Cross. In this death man, opening fully to grace, becomes a sharer in the divine nature. This can only happen by a relinquishment of the limited and limiting ego or "finite self." This relinquishment is also a liberation, the final freedom and the only true and absolute freedom. The seed dies and in dying becomes fully and joyfully all that lay dormant and constricted within it. This mystical death may coincide with physical death, but it does not seem that this is usually the case. St. John of the Cross seems to think that for many it has to await the purifying "fire" of Purgatory, while Eastern mysticism sees it as the culmination of many births and deaths. All one can say is that there can be no "easy way" towards this final fulfilment, for man must be transformed in his deepest conscious attitudes, in his radical will.[15] And we can say, further, that he who would prepare himself for this fulfilment must learn to look death in the face, seeing it at all levels, accepting the full meaning and symbolism of "Sister Death," inseparable companion of life.

[15]Speaking of this mystical death which he calls "night" St. John of the Cross says: "All that we can possibly say would fall far short of expressing what this night really is" (*The Dark Night*, ch. 7, par. 2).

Looking death in the face means looking mystical death in the face, and at times mystical death shows itself as radical annihilation of life, of all that self-life stands for. I have said that it is only the man who has a full sense of life, who has lived fully (which is another way of saying "the true mystic") who can have a full sense of this annihilation. Only he has, so to speak, the space within to open to that fullness of pathos and poignancy that marks the fullness of death and dying.

And at this point God is absent. Or if God is there, he is mysteriously detached or even more mysteriously uncaring. *My God my God why hast thou forsaken me?* Why? Why? Why?

There is no answer from the silent skies over Auschwitz (to use John Garvey's phrase), from the relentless ocean as the sharks speed forward. Some years ago a man and his wife and their three children had a car breakdown in the Australian desert, and nobody came. They were religious folk and they must have prayed, but nobody came. They died, one by one, all five of them. This is my death and yours, unless we would try somehow to cheat death, to scale it down to our own dimensions, to *domesticate* it. The mystic knows that this is the truth of death, that in such cases there is a coincidence of physical death and mystical death, that the death of the deepest Dark Night and this death in the desert are but aspects of a single human experience.

God is absent, but Christ is present. He has gone this way already into the Garden with its "horror and dismay," on to the fullness of the *Lamma Sabachthani.*

He is there, and of course all is well. *But not yet.* To follow Christ through this narrow gate is to be entirely alone, to share his very aloneness as he travels to the very end the road of love, as he becomes the fullest revelation of the love of the Son for the Father, as he reveals the mystery of the divine weakness that is the very power and glory of divine love. And in the face of this, the enquiring, speculative, theological mind must be silent. But the heart waits, sharing that "Solitude of Mary" which the Spaniards celebrate on Holy Saturday. In that solitude only love remains, and only love matters. And within that love, like a child in the womb, like a secret too sacred to be spoken, like a man by his own fireside, like a woman in her familiar kitchen, is Joy: substantial, enduring, indestructible.

11

Something Understood
Reflections on the Future
of Academic Theology

Church-Bells beyond the starres heard, the soul's bound,
the land of spices; something understood.

George Herbert: Prayer.

1

In the bad old days in which my theological training took place, it was assumed that the student had to apply himself to the study of logic before he studied theology, just as he was supposed to know Greek before he studied the New Testament, and Latin before he was accepted even as a theological toddler. I am not concerned here with contrasting this narrow-minded situation with that of our more liberated days in which everybody pontificates freely about everything, but only with reaching back in my memory for an illustration that appeared in the old books on Logic as an example of a dilemma. I am not concerned with the historical accuracy of the illustration, but only with its sharp and mighty horns; for those over 50 in my audience will remember that dilemmas had horns on which one got impaled unless he either grasped one of both horns like a lad of mettle, or else escaped craftily between them. Well, the dilemma supposedly recounted the judgement of a certain Caliph who ordered the burning of the great library of Alexandria; for, he said, these books either merely repeat something already in the Koran, or they contain matter not found in the Koran; in the first case they are superfluous; in the second case they are pernicious; so, since they are either superfluous or pernicious, the proper thing is to burn them. So, not for the first time nor the last, a simple believer struck a match on the *tabula rasa* of his mind, which destroyed all other sources of illumination.

I am not concerned here with the Koran, about which I know very little, but about the Christian Bible, that is to say the New Testament in itself and the Old Testament as its background and preparation. And I want to say that this book is great and sacred, indeed uniquely so, not only in the light it radiates but in the innumerable lights it reflects, that a study of Scripture which is not open at least in principle to all that men have thought and done, to every moment and aspect of the *admirabile commercium* between God and man, is not only inadequate but extremely dangerous. I am not attacking biblical fundamentalism, but rather explaining in what sense I am a biblical fundamentalist for whom the Bible is the source of all light and grace. Above all, I want to argue strongly that the wisdom of the Holy Book not only needs the library of many books to be fully itself, but also needs open independent academical institutions if it is to fulfil its purpose as a lamp to our feet in the dark and terrifying journey that lies ahead of us as we look over the crest of the second Christian millennium, look into that enormous and terrifying darkness which could well force us not to look at all.

Let me begin with an image. Sacred Scripture, the Holy Book is like a deep clear lake in the mountains: there are many such lakes in my native mountains in the South of Ireland, as also in the Scottish highlands. It is a marvellous experience to swim in such a lake; it is a special communion with the sky overhead and the hills all around, with the life that is every-where in all the wildness of wild life, with the challenging and exhilarating touch of the water itself. It is also an expressive and uplifting experience to stand by the lake and see the sky reflected within it, and the great mountains and, it may be, the works of man along its margin: house and hut and fold. Experiences such as these are good, and the lake lives a special life within those who meet it in this way allowing it to speak with all its voices, to open out to its full dimensions, above all leaving the way open to the infinity of air and sky, of the sun and the moon and the stars.

But it is also possible to lean over the lake at one particular point and to see first and last one's own reflection, to refuse to see the lake in any other way, to hold fast to the illusion that the whole lake has, so to speak, nothing to do but reflect this one image. The lake stands, of course, for the Holy Book; and there are many who bend over the Book in this way, seeing within it not the open countenance of the Word through whom all things are made, but rather the tight, self-righteous reflection of their own face. Such a man truly *incurvatus in se* can only protect himself by trying to impose this closed image on the whole world.

Do not think it is easy to get such a man to stand up straight and look at the lake in all its amplitude and beauty, to see the Holy Book as reflecting all human philosophy and human culture, to accept the vast variety of points of view that show forth the riches and glory of God's testament with men. St.

John Chrysostom used the word *synkatabasis* to express the divine considerateness, or, if you like, the divine tact in God's self-revelation to man. The word of God meets each man where he can receive it in the individual sanctuary of his heart. So, too, it meets different cultures differently, and different epochs. So, too, it has for each epoch its own special challenge to open to the holiness of God.

So it is that the story of the Holy Book of Christians is the story of Christendom, not only a history of the Church, East and West, but a history of the whole Western world. All this, however, from a special standpoint, as if one were to describe the sea and the mountains as reflected in a lake. In a sense this would be a history of the earthing of the heavenly book, a history of the incarnation of the Word of God. This history still remains to be written, though much of the material for it is lying around. We have histories of Christian art, Christian music, Christian literature, and in all this Sacred Scripture is indelibly and vividly present, but we do not easily consider how the artist, the musician, the poet give us a deeper reading, a deeper understanding, the joy and illumination of a special reflection *on* Scripture and *of* Scripture. So, too, we have histories of Christian philosophy, such as Gilson's, but they are all the other way round, as if the waters of philosophy reflected the peaks of theology, and of course this is legitimate from the point of view of a deeper understanding of philosophy. But it does not really help us much with our reading of Scripture. It does not begin to show us the depth, clarity, and beauty of Scripture as the mirror of man's mind at its deepest and highest.

Take for example the celebrated proof of God's existence enunciated by St. Anselm, which says in effect that there is no need for such a proof since the idea of God encloses all our affirmations of existence. I am not concerned here with the validity of this most subtle and simple piece of reasoning beyond saying that only the most immature type of student or the most senile type of professor dismisses it as a mere sophism. What concerns me is the controversy as to whether Anselm is speaking as a philosopher standing, so to speak, at the bar of reason or as a theologian who is in fact already assuming the existence of God as something amply affirmed in the Christian Scriptures. Karl Barth, a man about whom those of you who haven't heard will hear very soon, took the second alternative, and went on from there to build the most impressive theological system of modern times. Many commentators question his reading of Anselm, and say he is reading his own post-Kantian mind into that of a tenth century scholastic. If we remember that Anselm was trained in a great philosophical and theological tradition which carefully distinguished the two disciplines, and revelled in the subtle analyses in which the hinges of this distinction could be heard creaking—as much-used hinges tend to do—if we keep this background in mind it becomes clear that philosophical argument for Anselm always retains its contours and colours as philosophy, and is only of use as long as this is so, yet is, nevertheless, used as a powerful aid to the deeper understanding of Scripture. The word of God shines by its own light yet it marvellously reflects all other lights and by this reflection reveals its own depth and variety. The great achievement of the Irishman Scotus Eriugena (apart from appearing on Irish five pound notes) was to have described the mysterious sky of Neoplatonism as reflected in the infinite deep of the Holy Book; a few centuries later a Scotsman who has variously immortalised the little town of Duns from which he came, endeavoured with unbelievable comprehensiveness and subtlety to put all that marvellous interplay of light in one treatise; in between, the great Thomas of Aquin used the mighty mountain range of Aristotelian metaphysics to measure the immeasurable depths of what he called *Sapientia Divina*, the wisdom of God revealing itself to man in the Face of Christ.

One could call a roster of all the great philosopher-theologians to make the same point, and this roster would include Luther and Calvin. It is true that they felt that the word could be lost if too much attention were paid to the philosophy or philosophies it reflected, but they nevertheless accepted the heritage of a philosophy illuminative of theology. Some of my colleagues of the Church of Scotland are much embarrassed by the medieval flavour of the Westminster Confession with its rather uncomplimentary references to the Bishop of Rome, but I am hoping that it will remain, for it clearly affirms the thesis of the immortality of the soul, which is a Platonic philosophical doctrine deeply and clearly reflected in Scripture for the Fathers and the medieval theologians, Catholic and Reformed. As I see it, the uncomplimentary references to the Bishop of Rome may perhaps lead to the death of men, but 'the rejection of the philosophical thesis announces the death of man.

Perhaps I have said enough to illustrate my vision of the reflective quality of the word of God as set down in the Holy Book of all Christians. The same point could be made in terms of literature, music, painting. Who that truly loves and lives the Scriptures can read or see Shakespeare's *King Lear*, or any great play, without returning to the Holy Book with a clearer and deeper vision of the ways of God with man, and the pathos and poignancy of man's condition? Who can listen to

Bach or to Handel without some deepening of his Christian consciousness and a fuller understanding of the sacred text? As for painting, architecture and the rest it is obvious that the arts of line, shape, structure and colour are essential to the incarnation of the word of God in a world of line, shape, structure and colour. We cannot choose to do without the artist; all we can do is choose between good artists and bad artists. And I doubt whether we are in this matter any better than our fathers.

2

Here in New College we have a celebrated theological library which is part of the library complex of the University of Edinburgh. If you visit New College Library you will find several sections devoted to Biblical Literature, and in one section you will find, copies of the Bible itself in the original Greek and Hebrew. At the centre of this nucleus is the Greek New Testament, and every student of theology should have access to this, should master enough Greek to meet it in its native dress, should do this even if he has to stay up all night twice a week. This is the centre, at once a lamp and a mirror, illuminating and reflecting all around, first the place of origins, the land of sunrise, of the Old Testament and all that surrounds it, then the great valleys of Patristics, the world of the Fathers and their adversaries, all men of the Holy Book, some of them fighting great battles to possess it. Further on is the great panorama of Christian and secular history, a world which some find sufficient to itself. Finally there are the great mountains and forests of philosophy, some of the mountains well-nigh inaccessible, some of the forests well-nigh impenetrable. Of course there is much else in our library, much that has to do with worship, with communication, much that builds bridges towards other disciplines. Indeed these bridging sections remind us that as our Faculty is an integral part of the structure of a great university, so our library is part of the great world of university books in Edinburgh and beyond. It is the world of "whatever is of good report," of all man's honest thinking and inspired imagining, and it is all reflected in the limpid depths of the Holy Book. Not only that but it of human history and of man's continuing, painful, exhilarating encounter with himself.

I am and shall, I hope, always remain a biblical fundamentalist, for whom the words of Bible shine with dazzling light. But this light is not only dazzling, it is also deep, quiet, reflective. Look at the eyes of the man who is merely a preacher, who carries around that gleam in the eye that can perhaps hypnotise vast congregations. Such a man may indeed wake people from sleep, but he cannot lead them out to green pastures. Look at the eyes of the man or woman who has pondered the word of God in his heart night and day, see that depth, that peace, that contemplative quietness and gentleness. Such a man or woman has caught some of the deeper radiance of Scripture, and it is this deeper radiance that ultimately reveals itself through theological education. The narrow ultimately aggressive gleam in the eye has become the quiet warm glowing radiance of Christian understanding. If such a man is a preacher he is truly a living witness to the word of God, a true servant of the Living Word.

The world today has largely lost its soul, and is on the way to losing its mind, has indeed already lost its mind. Scientific materialism as a philosophy of life has finally looked straight at man, and its pitiless gaze has turned him to stone. So we await the nuclear holocaust, and prepare for it with all due scientific precision. In such an atmosphere it is well to have preachers, even if the gleam in the eye is as shallow as it is dazzling. They serve like the geese in Ancient Rome to awaken the people. But the need for preahcers and latter-day prophets does not diminish but rather accentuates the need for centres of theological education, where the deeper light of Scripture is carefully and reverently explored, questioned, related to philosophy and culture, to literature and art, above all where the word of God is seen in relation to the heart of man in all its dimensions.

The various Christian denominations have always felt the need for such centres, and the world is full of Bible Colleges, Catholic Seminaries and the rest, and some of them are given the name of universities. In such institutions there can be, in varying degrees, a genuine study of the text and context of the word of God, but at some stage this is limited by the need for the particular church or sect to find its own face reflected in Scripture. For this purpose a few texts are singled out as best reflecting the position of the group, and all other texts are made to reflect these few texts. So it comes that the greater part of Scripture is neither allowed to shine with its own light nor to reflect anything of philosophy or literature; it is allowed to reflect only the few texts approved by the group. These texts at the beginning may have sparked off some liberating insight in some founding father, but now they represent a trapped light that can never open out to the light from other stars, even when these stars shine clearly in the depths of that very Scripture which they claim to venerate.

Not all denominational schools, colleges or universities so-called go as far as this in imprisoning the word of God, but there is somewhere a closing-down point in all such institutions, and it is the word of God that suffers.

A real university faculty is quite different, works on an entirely different principle. If it is a Christian faculty it will indeed centre on the Bible, but it will not expect an individual teacher to obey any other law than that of searching for the truth of the text, nor to adopt any other standards than those of academic honesty and excellence. In such an atmosphere the students commitment will be respected whether he be Protestant Evangelical, or Eastern Orthodox, or Roman Catholic or Anglican, or even if he has no Christian commitment at all. If the university is working well he will gain most from confrontation with his fellow-students: this is something which no correspondence-style or "open" university can give. Neither, of course, can it give that availability of teachers to students, which means not only creative confrontation, but also the opening up of avenues for the student as he discovers how his newest thoughts have been echoed by the great men of the past.

Here I touch on the question of tradition, admitting by the way that I am not only a fundamentalist but a traditionalist. Tradition in the context of university education is all that has been handed down, all that is stored on the shelves of our libraries, all that is from ancient days of good report. The university is the guardian and repository, the agent and dispenser of the marvellous riches of tradition. What is most terrifying about recent government policy on British universities is the complete lack of appreciation that a country that loses its universities is like a man that loses his memory, that a modern state without a strong university presence will be in a position far worse than that of a primitive people who have at least enclosed there memory in ritual and folklore. We are on the way to becoming a country without a past, and a country without a past is a country without a future. It is true that

Britain has in practice gone only a short distance down this road, but let it be said that it would not have gone this far in practice had it not gone the whole way in principle. We will of course continue to have schools of professional studies, but I greatly fear that most of our rulers, and many of our practical academics, have simply not enough room in their heads for the *idea* of a university.

In this climate theology easily comes to be seen as dispensable, especially as many Christians of goodwill are persuaded by their own Church leaders that what is most needed is centres of indoctrination, that univesity theology is dangerously liberal, and can blunt the edge of truly committed candidates for the ministry or priesthood. I have been arguing that this attitude is ultimately destructive of the Bible in all its power and amplitude, that it is a disastrous mistake to think we can leave the understanding and communication of the word of God to the men of closed countenance, to the preachers with the gleam in the eye whether they be Protestant, Catholic or Latter-day Saints. I have been, in effect, saying that the theological enterprise in which we are engaged here in the Faculty of Divinity of the University of Edinburgh is a high and holy work without which the land will be laid waste, as every man shouts his own way to salvation and no man ponders in his heart.

3

After two thousand years the most striking and paradoxical fact about Christianity is that it is deeply fragmented. The name of Jesus is a name of division, even a name of hatred, for people hate and despise each other in the name of that name by which every knee should bend. Again and again, earnest, even holy, people have tried to start afresh, to capture that first vision of a people united, sharing, loving one another in the name of the man who loved his own even into death. Alas, all that came of these efforts was a further fragmentation, a new denomination to add to those already in the field. Of course each fragment is convinced thta it represents the truth, that it alone is Christian, pointing out either that it is the largest fragment; or the most ancient, or the only fragment that can truly read the Holy Book. Each fragment has its own saints, most of them, if not all, have their own well-attested miracles, for truly these divisions reach at least as far as the First Heaven.

It is indeed good to have variety, and I would not on any account have us all dressed the same way, or singing the same songs, or even breaking bread according to one ritual. But variety is one thing, discord another. It is one thing to talk to one another and to listen to one another; it is another to shout and hurl anathemas at each other, to push and jostle over the Holy Sepulchre of the Risen Christ.

Now there is only one place or kind of institution on the face of the earth where all denominations and all religions can meet, and that is a university faculty of theology. This in our culture will, as I have said, be a Christian faculty whose primary constituency will be the Christian world and whose primary professional clientele will be Christian ministers, though its primary purpose will not be ministerial training, but the common pursuit of Christian understanding, the common task of interpreting the Holy Book, the perservation of the vast heritage of our common Christian past. Within this setting of a common commitment to the truth, a common readiness to face all facts and follow all arguments, there will be place for a Department of Religion in which non-Christian religions are studied according to available resources—here there are obvious bridges to other faculties and departments within the university. What I am describing here is the situation in our Faculty of Divinity, which over the past fifteen years or so has been first reaching out to include all Christian denominations, and over the past five years has been reaching out to other religions. Some Presbyterians have seen this as a threat to the teaching of their own ministers, but I challenge anybody to produce any real evidence that the Presbyterian students have been any the poorer for all this in their commitment to the Gospel of Christ. Neither has any Episcopalian or Roman Catholic student suffered any diminishment in their deepest commitments to the Gospel as mediated by his own denomination. Rather has this diversity of presences helped to heal the breach between fundamentalists and liberals within the various denominations: it is not so easy to get fully excited about a family quarrel when interested onlookers are asking to please explain what it's all about.

Christianity today all over the planet is faced with the problems of healing the past and liberating the future, healing the past of its dark poison of hatred that still runs in our veins, liberating the future from sectarian prejudice and possessiveness, allowing Christian men and women to read the Holy Book together, not bending over some backwater seeing one's own reflexion, but seeing the vast reaches of these waters as they reflect all man's history and all his enterprises and glories, all his pain too, and the great Dragon that now stands on the shore of the sea. More and more Christians are being suddenly confronted with this Dragon of Nuclear War which should really be called the Destroyer whose wound is worse than death. We know for instance that it is better to live in Glasgow than Edinburgh, for Glasgow will be the place of annihilating first strike, and the people of the East Coast will die slowly and painfully of fall-out. We see the Dragon, and we are forced to face it together, Catholic, Protestant, Jew, Muslim.

We have in fact the weapon to destroy it, a weapon that lies, like Excalibur, in the depths of those deep dark waters. It was the sword used by the Master himself, a sword which few men since his time have been strong enough to use. For no man can use it unless it has first pierced his own heart. This sword he left with his disciples when he went away to be with them more deeply. He called it Peace; it is the Sword of Peace. It is the most terrible weapon in the world. He who wields it must turn the other cheek, not slavishly but implacably. There is nothing more terrible than the other cheek; there is nothing more utterly piercing than the Sword of Peace.

I am not calling for any simple-minded pacifism, but for a full understanding of that Peace which lies hidden in the heart of the Christian Gospel. This can be reached only by a deep meditation at once scriptural, historical, psychological, philosophical. It can be achieved only by a reinstatement and restatement of Christian ethics. Above all it can only be reached by those who pray with Christ in quiet places.

But it can be done, and it must be done. For the Dragon will not go away. And it can only be done if all Christians learn to look again at the Holy Book in its full dimensions and its full demands. This is first and always a task for theology in the University, theology in the context of science, technology, history and the rest, theology as conscious of its responsibility to the past and to the future. But this theology must unite within its fold all Christians who are ready to talk to their fellow Christians, ready to read the Holy Book together, and discover those treasures hidden within it which alone can save the world.

4

I have spoken much of the Holy Book assuming that we all know what I mean, that we all have a copy of it. But it has two main parts, and there may be some ambiguity as regards their relationship. Let me say, then, that for me, the Holy Book of Christians is the New Testament in itself, and the Old Testament as seen from the standpont of the New. This is not to deny that the Old Testament may be legitimately seen from other standpoints, by the Jew, the Muslim, or the philosopher of religion. In the Christian perspective the Old Testament not only provides the background of the New but forms with it a marvellous unity of prayer and reflection. Essentially the New Testament tells the story of a man whose death changed the inner substance of our planet, a man who called himself the Living Bread that gives *aeonic* life to men. As this Bread of Life dips down into the dark and twisted cosmos where Satan rules, and is received by man it becomes utterly broken; so, too, the blood flows freely as wine from the wine-press. All this and more that became fact on Calvary was already there as symbol in the Old Testament, as if it were an orchestra already assembled waiting for the Master musician to make it live. So it is that the accounts of the death of Jesus Christ are all meditations taken directly from the Old Testament, from Isaiah and the Psalms particularly. In his death, as in his life, Jesus is living through an ancient mystery of prayer, of man reaching towards the heavens, and of the Lord of Spirits overshadowing man, typically in Moses and Elias, typically also in Abraham, the man of faith, and in Mary of Nazareth who believed and pondered in her heart the mystery of her son.

Jesus of Nazareth as he comes before us in the Holy Book was not a man who healed and preached and worked miracles and *also* spent time in prayer. No; prayer as constant vital communion with the Father was the inner breath of his being, "the pulse of his heart," to use the Gaelic phrase that lovers have used from time immemorial. It is in prayer especially that we glimpse the Holy Trinity or Triunity, the *Perichoresis* or sacred dance of which the Fathers speak, all-fathering love received by the Son who is also the bride, and that breathing of love which is eternally its own ground in the common ground of That-Which-Is-Eternally.

Here is something understood that is always being more deeply understood, that is never finally understood. What opens up before us is the mystery of prayer, the contemplative dimension where all reflection has its proper space. We can legitimately try to look into this mystery as in theology we look into all mysteries. But a mystery cannot be pushed away and objectified; it must be welcomed, appropriated, lived in everyday life. Only thus through living participation can that which is something understood become the ground of creativity, of philosophical-theological insight, of poetry, of art, become a way into that most transcendent and fulfilling of all human occupations, the Worship of the Living God.

So it is that prayer, meditation, worship is an essential element in the life of a theological institute. So it is that in New College we have a worship time together each day, and a few days each year devoted to the common sharing in the prayer of Christ. So it is that the Worship Committee has a central role in the life of our faculty.

In a sense all is well here; yet I feel that we need to take stock of the situation, and realise that the challenge of our fragmented Christendom, and the fact that we are face to face with the Nuclear Dragon, demands more than we provide. What we need to look at especially is the exclusiveness of the larger denominations in this matter, Church of Scotland, Episcopalian, Roman Catholic. I would appeal to these and other denominations to ask themselves whether their students come here merely to study, or whether they also come here to pray and to share the living prayer-presence of Christ with their fellow-Christians and others. Are we in our denominational enclave really and truly convinced that we do it better on our own? If we think this, perhaps we should look a little more closely at the parable of the Pharisee and the Publican. Our fellow-Christians may well be benighted, but the God we worship shows an extraordinary interest in the benighted.

I think we should also reach out to the other faculties and departments in the University, perhaps inviting people in the first instance to lead our midday worship. This need not cut across, but should rather build up with what is already provided by the various chaplaincies. I feel that what comes from within the academic world itself has a special relevance for the academic community. Our Faculty here is unusual among theological faculties in its involvement at the administrative level in the university community, and this should also show itself at the level of prayer and worship. We are not ashamed of a Gospel that reflects and illuminates all aspects of human investigation and human endeavour.

One final point before I leave this topic of prayer and worship. It seems to me that the increasing number of women studying theology has notably enriched the prayer-consciousness of our community. Certainly it is my experience that when a woman leads the midday worship she does so very sensitively and helpfully, perhaps because she sees it as very important. Perhaps the future of the world depends on prayer, on our identification with the prayer of Christ and that in this matter women must lead rather than follow. We know that St. Paul found it hard to cope with feminine energies in his communities, though Christ himself had no such difficulty. Again, this is a matter where the Holy Book easily and deeply reflects a profound change of consciousness on the part of Western man, the consciousness that the masculine and feminine must work together to build a new world. In the ancient legend it was the women who guarded Excalibur. Perhaps it is through the woman's voice in theology that Christ's powerful Word of Peace will be heard again and the Sword of Peace recovered from the depths of our Christ-consciousness.

5

I have tried to give imaginative substance to this talk by way of one central image, an image taken from the mountains of Kerry in the South of Ireland where I grew up. It is the image of a lake among the hills, as it might be Loch Acoose or Luascanach, each small and set among the mountains and the wild uplands. Or it might be the much larger Lakes of Killarney, a whole wide expanding valley of lake and woodland, mountain-girt and ringed with the stately homes of long ago, well-furnished with islands and little bays and mountain-streams, tumbling down. I have fixed on one main aspect of all these lakes, little and great, their reflective quality as they receive sky and mountain and woodland and habitation into their depths. I have used this image to illustrate a great truth which does not depend on any image, the truth that Sacred Scripture is a book open to all human life, to philosophy and literature, to cultural shocks and changes. In our own day the real achievement of Barth, Bultmann, Rahner and Teilhard, if I may be allowed to spancel together these great names, was to show that in a time of the shaking of the foundations the Holy Book could reflect man's situation however variously analysed or understood, could reflect the human predicament in its pages and illuminate the past, the present and the future. So I say to the student coming in: when you see these serried ranks of the *Church Dogmatics* and the rest, do not quail or feel that you may sink without trace; for it is all there in the familiar Bible you bring with you. It is all there but not if you grasp the Bible too tightly, or get impaled on the horns of that famous dilemma of the Caliph at Alexandria. It is all there, but as an invitation to life, to all the wonders of the life of the mind, the heart, the imagination.

Perhaps I may be allowed to recall my image one last time. The man who gazes earnestly into one corner of the lake sees all the time his own image; the man who takes always the large view sees many wonders reflected in the waters. But the invitation is not only to gaze, but to stoop down very low and drink of the Living Waters. That is the way of prayer and worship and the peace of Christ.